PROMISES AND BEGINNINGS

Examining Excellence in the Creator's Ways

A Study in the Book of Genesis

Jack W. Hayford

with
Joseph Snider

THOMAS NELSON PUBLISHERS
Nashville

CONTENTS

∎ ∎

Promises and Beginnings: Examining Excellence in the Creator's Ways (A Study in the Book of Genesis) is one of a series of study guides that focus exciting, discovery-geared coverage of Bible book and power themes—all prompting toward dynamic, Holy Spirit-filled living.

About the Executive Editor

JACK W. HAYFORD, noted pastor, teacher, writer, and composer, is the Executive Editor of the complete series, working with the publisher in the conceiving and developing of each of the books.

Dr. Hayford is Senior Pastor of The Church On The Way, the First Foursquare Church of Van Nuys, California. He and his wife, Anna, have four married children, all of whom are active in either pastoral ministry or vital church life. As General Editor of the *Spirit-Filled Life Bible*, Pastor Hayford led a four-year project, which has resulted in the availability of one of today's most practical and popular study Bibles. He is author of more than twenty books, including *A Passion for Fullness, The Beauty of Spiritual Language, Rebuilding the Real You,* and *Prayer Is Invading the Impossible.* His musical compositions number over four hundred songs, including the widely sung "Majesty."

About the Writer

JOSEPH SNIDER has worked in Christian ministry for twenty-two years. In addition to freelance writing and speaking, he worked three years with Young Life, served for seven years on the Christian Education faculty at Fort Wayne Bible College, and pastored churches in Indianapolis and Fort Wayne, Indiana. He currently enjoys part-time teaching at Franklin College in Franklin, Indiana. His writing includes material for Thomas Nelson Publishers, Moody Magazine, Union Gospel Press, and David C. Cook.

Married to Sally Snider, Joe has two children: Jenny is 21 and Ted is 18. They live in Indianapolis, Indiana. Joe earned a B.A. in English from Cedarville College in Cedarville, Ohio, and a Th.M. in Christian Education from Dallas Theological Seminary.

Of this contributor, the Executive Editor has remarked: "Joe Snider's strength and stability as a gracious, godly man comes through in his writing. His perceptive and practical way of pointing the way to truth inspires students of God's Word."

THE GIFT THAT KEEPS ON GIVING

Who doesn't like presents? Whether they come wrapped in colorful paper and beautiful bows, or brown paper bags closed and tied at the top with old shoestring. Kids and adults of all ages love getting and opening presents.

But even this moment of surprise and pleasure can be marked by dread and fear. All it takes is for these words to appear: "Assembly Required. Instructions Enclosed." How we hate these words! They taunt us, tease us, beckon us to try to challenge them, all the while knowing that they have the upper hand. If we don't understand the instructions, or if we ignore them and try to put the gift together ourselves, more than likely we'll only assemble frustration and anger. What we felt about our great gift all the joy, anticipation, and wonder—will vanish. And they will never return, at least not to that pristine state they had before we realized that *we* had to assemble our present with instructions *no consumer* will ever understand.

One of the most precious gifts God has given us is His Word, the Bible. Wrapped in the glory and sacrifice of His Son and delivered by the power and ministry of His Spirit, it is a treasured gift—one the family of God has preserved and protected for centuries as a family heirloom. It promises that it is the gift that keeps on giving, because the Giver it reveals is inexhaustible in His love and grace.

Tragically, though, fewer and fewer people, even those who number themselves among God's everlasting family, are opening this gift and seeking to understand what it's all about and how to use it. They often feel intimidated by it. It requires some assembly, and its instructions are hard to comprehend sometimes. How does the Bible fit together anyway?

What does Genesis have to do with Revelation? Who are Abraham and Moses, and what is their relationship to Jesus and Paul? And what about the works of the Law and the works of faith? What are they all about, and how do they fit together, if at all?

And what does this ancient Book have to say to us who are looking toward the twenty-first century? Will taking the time and energy to understand its instructions and to fit it all together really help you and me? Will it help us better understand who we are, what the future holds, how we can better live here and now? Will it really help us in our personal relationships, in our marriages and families, in our jobs? Can it give us more than just advice on how to handle crises? the death of a loved one? the financial fallout of losing a job? catastrophic illness? betrayal by a friend? the seduction of our values? the abuses of the heart and soul? Will it allay our fears and calm our restlessness and heal our wounds? Can it really get us in touch with the same power that gave birth to the universe? that parted the Red Sea? that raised Jesus from the stranglehold of the grave? Can we really find unconditional love, total forgiveness, and genuine healing in its pages?

Yes. Yes. Without a shred of doubt.

The *Spirit-Filled Life Bible Discovery Guide* series is designed to help you unwrap, assemble, and enjoy all God has for you in the pages of Scripture. It will focus your time and energy on the books of the Bible, the people and places they describe, and the themes and life applications that flow thick from its pages like honey oozing from a beehive.

So you can get the most out of God's Word, this series has a number of helpful features. Each study guide has no more than fourteen lessons, each arranged so you can plumb the depths or skim the surface, depending on your needs and interests.

The study guides also contain six major sections, each marked by a symbol and heading for easy identification.

 WORD WEALTH

The WORD WEALTH feature provides important definitions of key terms.

BEHIND THE SCENES

BEHIND THE SCENES supplies information about cultural beliefs and practices, doctrinal disputes, business trades, and the like, that illuminate Bible passages and teachings.

 AT A GLANCE

The AT A GLANCE feature uses maps and charts to identify places and simplify themes or positions.

 BIBLE EXTRA

Because this study guide focuses on a book of the Bible, you will find a BIBLE EXTRA feature that guides you into Bible dictionaries, Bible encyclopedias, and other resources that will enable you to glean more from the Bible's wealth if you want something extra.

 PROBING THE DEPTHS

Another feature, PROBING THE DEPTHS, will explain controversial issues raised by particular lessons and cite Bible passages and other sources to which you can turn to help you come to your own conclusions.

 FAITH ALIVE

Finally, each lesson contains a FAITH ALIVE feature. Here the focus is, So what? Given what the Bible says, what does it mean for my life? How can it impact my day-to-day needs, hurts, relationships, concerns, and whatever else is important to me? FAITH ALIVE will help you see and apply the practical relevance of God's literary gift.

As you'll see, these guides supply space for you to answer the study and life-application questions and exercises. You may, however, want to record all your answers, or just the overflow from your study or application, in a separate notebook or journal. This would be especially helpful if you think you'll dig into the BIBLE EXTRA features. Because the exercises in this feature are optional and can be expanded as far as you want to take them, we have not allowed writing space for them in this study guide. So you may want to have a notebook or journal handy for recording your discoveries while working through to this feature's riches.

The Bible study method used in this series revolves around four basic steps: observation, interpretation, correlation, and application. Observation answers the question, What does the text say? Interpretation deals with, What does the text mean?—not with what it means to you or me, but what it meant to its original readers. Correlation asks, What light do other Scripture passages shed on this text? And application, the goal of Bible study, poses the question, How should my life change in response to the Holy Spirit's teaching of this text?

If you have used a Bible much before, you know that it comes in a variety of translations and paraphrases. Although you can use any of them with profit as you work through the *Spirit-Filled Life Bible Discovery Guide* series, when Bible passages or words are cited, you will find they are from the New King James Version of the Bible. Using this translation with this series will make your study easier, but it's certainly not necessary.

The only resources you need to complete and apply these study guides are a heart and mind open to the Holy Spirit, a prayerful attitude, and a pencil and a Bible. Of course, you may draw upon other sources, such as commentaries, dictionaries, encyclopedias, atlases, and concordances, and you'll even find some optional exercises that will guide you into these sources. But these are extras, not necessities. These study guides are comprehensive enough to give you all you need to gain a good, basic understanding of the Bible book being covered and how you can apply its themes and counsel to your life.

A word of warning, though. By itself, Bible study will not transform your life. It will not give you power, peace, joy, comfort, hope, and a number of other gifts God longs for you to unwrap and enjoy. Through Bible study, you will grow in your understanding of the Lord, His kingdom and your place in it, and those things are essential. But you need more. You need to rely on the Holy Spirit to guide your study and your application of the Bible's truths. He, Jesus promised, was sent to teach us "all things" (John 14:26; cf. 1 Cor. 2:13). So as you use this series to guide you through Scripture, bathe your study time in prayer, asking the Spirit of God to illuminate the text, enlighten your mind, humble your will, and comfort your heart. He will never let you down.

My prayer and goal for you is that as you unwrap and begin to explore God's Book for living His way, the Holy Spirit will fill every fiber of your being with the joy and power God longs to give all His children. So read on. Be diligent. Stay open and submissive to Him. You will not be disappointed. He promises you!

Lesson 1/In the Beginning God Promised

I love to work jigsaw puzzles, but you don't want to be around me when I do. I become unsociable and irritable as the puzzle absorbs all my attention.

I work puzzles incorrectly, too. I don't want to sort out the pieces and construct the border first. I dump out the puzzle, turn over a bunch of pieces, collect all the ones with bright colors on them, and begin assembling the picture in several places at once.

In a while, I've put together all the easily recognizable portions of the picture and arranged them on my work surface in approximately the right relationships to the space the completed puzzle will occupy. That phase of working a puzzle goes quickly, and I like it.

Then the problem is that all the rest of the pieces, easily three-quarters of the total, are either blue for water or sky and green for grass or trees. At that point, I have to break down and sort out all the border pieces and construct the framework. Then, and only then, can I grumble and complain my way to another picture of that lighthouse in Maine or that village in Vermont with the covered bridge and the Methodist church. You know the ones I mean.

For many people, studying the Old Testament is like my adventures in working jigsaw puzzles. There are some stories in there that are familiar from Sunday school days, like the bright patches of color in the puzzle scene. In between the familiar stories are long stetches of unfamiliar narrative and lists of names that seem as featureless as the sky or the grass in the puzzle.

Before you tackle Genesis, looking for the bright patches of familiar stories, let's construct the framework so you can see how the whole composition goes together to convey a message from God to the children of Israel in days gone by and from God to you today.

WHAT THE BIBLE SUGGESTS ABOUT GENESIS

Genesis presents itself anonymously. No author's name or date of composition is attached. But Genesis is the background every Israelite needed in order to understand their national history recorded in Exodus, Leviticus, Numbers, and Deuteronomy. These five books go together. To whom did Jesus attribute the writing of the first five books of the Old Testament? (Luke 16:29, 31; John 5:45–47)

Within the Pentateuch (the first five books of the Old Testament) are allusions to occasions when Moses wrote all or parts of three of them: Exodus (17.14; 24:4, 7), Numbers (33:1, 2), and Deuteronomy (31:9–13). In addition, Leviticus identifies itself as a record of the Lord's words to Moses (1:1).

Moses is not identified as the writer of Genesis within the Pentateuch. However, the only Old Testament account of the regulations and procedures of circumcision occurs in Genesis 17:9–14. In Acts 15:1 this teaching is called "the custom of Moses."

How many years before King Solomon built the temple did Moses lead the Israelites out of Egypt? (1 Kin. 6:1) _____. If the fourth year of Solomon's reign was about 996 B.C.[1], what was the approximate date of the Exodus? _____. If Moses compiled Genesis sometime during the next forty years while the Israelites wandered in the wilderness, what would be the latest it could have been written? _____ (Remember, when you move backward in time dated B.C. the numbers get larger, and when you move forward the numbers get smaller).

BEHIND THE SCENES

The Hebrew Bible has a simple way of naming its first five books. It uses the first word of each book as the name. What we call Genesis is named "Bereshith," which means "in the beginning." When the Old Testament was translated into Greek about 250 years before Christ, these books were given formal titles that reflected their content. The first book was titled Genesis, a Greek word for "origins" or "history."[2] This Greek name has become the standard name for the first book of the Old Testament in English translations.

THE STRUCTURE OF GENESIS

Genesis divides into two unequal halves. Chapters 1—11 recounts the spiritual history of the human race from Creation to the time of Abraham. These chapters reveal why God called out one man and began dealing in a unique way with his descendants. The larger section, chapters 12—50, tells the stories of the ancestors of Israel up to the time they moved to Egypt.

The context of the whole development of Genesis suggests overviewing it in three sections. The first section is the first "half" of the book (chs. 1—11), which narrates how the physical and social worlds came to be. The second section is the first part of the second "half" of the book (chs. 12—36), which tells how God selected Abraham, Isaac, and Jacob to initiate His chosen people. And the third section is the remainder of Genesis (chs. 37—50), which details how God purified the sons of Jacob to serve as patriarchs for the tribes of the nation Israel.

THE PROMISE OF EXISTENCE

Genesis 1—11 records the faithfulness of God the Creator to His creation in spite of the faithlessness of men and women. Look up the Genesis passages below and write down God's actions as the faithful Creator who insured the existence of the physical or social world.

1:1–31

BIBLE EXTRA

The necessary beginning point in studying the theme of "the kingdom of God" is the Bible's opening verse. Here we meet the Sovereign of all the Universe, whose <u>realm, reign,</u> and <u>regency</u> are described at the outset. 1) His <u>realm</u> (or scope of His rule) is transcendent; that is, not only does it include the entire physical universe, but it exceeds it. . . . 2) His <u>reign</u> (or the power by which He rules) is exercised by His will, His word, and His works. . . . 3) His <u>regency</u> (or authority to rule) is in His preexistence and holiness. All kingdom power and authority flow from Him.[3]

4:1–15

6:13–22

8:20—9:17

10:1–32

THE PROMISE OF RELATIONSHIP

In Genesis 12—36, God reveals Himself as the God who enters a covenant with a chosen family of faith. Look up the Genesis passages that follow and write down God's action to initiate or preserve a relationship with His chosen family.

11:31—12:9

15:1–21

17:1–27

18:16–33

21:1–21

22:1–19

24:1–67

25:19–34

28:10–22

31:3–18

32:9–32

35:1–15

 BIBLE EXTRA

The promise of God to Abraham that he would be "heir of the world" (Rom. 4:13) is repeated to his offspring, Isaac and Jacob, in succession. God's words and dealings in the lives of the patriarchs reveal that His unfolding program of redemption is dual. . . . He not only provides for restored fellowship with Himself (relationship), but covenants for human fulfillment and personal fruitfulness in life. This plan is geared not only to bless His people, but to make them a blessing to others.[4]

THE PROMISE OF SANCTIFICATION

Although Jacob was a man of absolute faith in the Lord who had revealed Himself at Bethel and blessed his life, he was also a deceitful man who raised a family of treacherous and violent sons (see, for example, Gen. 34). Before God would build a nation of the twelve sons of Jacob, He set out to make godly men of them through suffering.

Genesis 37—50 reveals this process of sanctification. Look at the Genesis passages below and write down what each reveals about (1) the wicked character of Jacob's sons, (2) suffering God allowed one or more of Jacob's sons to endure, or (3) righteousness produced in one or more of Jacob's sons because of suffering.

37:12–35

38:1–26

39:1—40:23

42:1–24

42:36—43:15; 46:1–34

45:1–15

50:15–21

 BEHIND THE SCENES

"Joseph's tests of his brothers were important in God's plan to channel his blessings through the seed of Abraham. God had planned to bring the family to Egypt so that it might grow into a great nation. But because the people who would form that nation had to be faithful, the brothers needed to be tested before they could share in the blessings. Joseph's prodding had to be subtle; the brothers had to perceive that God was moving against them so that they would acknowledge their crime against Joseph and demonstrate that they had changed."[5]

FAITH ALIVE

The Lord is the Creator. He is the God of beginnings. And He is the Lord of promises. He is ever faithful to His creatures who come to Him in faith for deliverance from eternal punishment for sin and from the power of sin in their daily lives.

What are some examples of how the Lord has been a faithful Creator to you, keeping His promises by protecting and preserving your physical existence?

What are some examples of how the Lord has assured you of His faithfulness, keeping His promises by maintaining His relationship with you as your Savior and Lord?

What are some examples of how the Lord has worked faithfully in and through the difficulties of your life to keep His promises by building holiness in your character?

1. Ronald Youngblood, *How It All Began* (Ventura, CA: Regal Books, 1980), 16.
2. Ibid., 11.
3. *Spirit-Filled Life Bible* (Nashville, TN: Thomas Nelson Publishers, 1991), 3, 4, "Kingdom Dynamics: God's Sovereignty."
4. Ibid., 43.
5. Allen P. Ross, *Creation and Blessing* (Grand Rapids, MI: Baker Book House, 1988), 647.

Lesson 2/The Beginning of All Things
(1:1—2:25)

James Weldon Johnson, a gifted Afro-American poet, songwriter, educator, attorney, statesman, and civil rights leader of the early twentieth century, published a book of seven poetic sermons entitled *God's Trombones*. Perhaps the best-known poem from that volume—"The Creation"—captures with a breathtaking interplay of power and gentleness how amazing it is that God Almighty is tenderly affectioned for a creature of clay.

Never mind that the details of the poem about how and why God created the universe differ from the biblical account. Just don't miss as you examine the first two chapters of Genesis the truth of Johnson's poem that God loved His human creations, that He got right down with them in intimate contact. And He still does.

MANKIND'S COSMIC ENVIRONMENT

The Bible begins with a bang. God didn't have Moses begin slowly and build up to the first main point. No. The first sentence of the Bible jumps with both feet on Creation, and the second sentence is off and running in high gear to expand on that opening summary. Answer the following questions from Genesis 1:1.

When did the Creation occur?

Who did the creating?

What did He create?

Answer the following questions from Genesis 1:2:

What was the condition of the earth that prompted God's creative work?

What was God's contact with the unstructured earth?

     BIBLE EXTRA

The Creation is an important biblical theme in more places than Genesis. In the Old Testament some passages you might want to look at and study in the future are Job 38, Psalm 104, and Isaiah 40:18–23; 42:5, 6. These texts do more than retell the Creation story. The writers reason from the Creation to its implication for our relationship to God.

In the New Testament the Lord reveals how the Son of God acted in Creation. Some passages to consider are John 1:1–13; Colossians 1:15–20; and Hebrews 1:1–3.

The six creative days address the problem that "the earth was without form, and void," that is, the earth was shapeless and empty. In the first three days God created the "forms," the broad categories of existence. In the second three days God addressed the emptiness of the earth by populating the vacant forms of the first three days.

Fill out the following chart by listing what God spoke into existence each day. Notice the relationships between days one through three and days four through six of the creative week.

FORM	FILLING
Day 1 _____	Day 4 _____
(Gen. 1:3–5)	(Gen. 1:14–19)
Day 2 _____	Day 5 _____
(Gen. 1:6–8)	(Gen. 1:20–23)
Day 3 _____	Day 6 _____
(Gen. 1:9–13)	(Gen. 1:24–31)

WORD WEALTH

The Hebrew verb *bara'*, translated "to create" in Genesis 1, means to make or to fashion. It can mean to bring into existence, as when God said, "Let there be light" (Gen. 1:3), and it can mean to work with existing material, as when God made man from the dust of the ground (2:7).

The unique feature of *bara'* in the Bible is that God is always the subject of this verb in its standard form. By reserving this word to describe God's creativity, the Scripture makes clear that divine and human creativity are different. The noblest human creation is but an after ripple of the original divine one described in Genesis 1 and 2.

From Genesis 1:27–30, what can you observe about man and woman in each of the following areas?

Their relationship to the image of God

Their relationship to the earth

Their relationship to other living creatures

Their relationship to plant life

 BIBLE EXTRA

"The image of God" (Gen. 1:27) that men and women bear does not involve physical appearance. It has to do with personality and the ability to form loving, committed relationships to other people and to God.

"God" in Genesis 1 is both singular and plural (v. 26), and so is "man" (v. 27). Men and women bear God's image individually, but in loving, committed relationships they show the complexity of God and humanity. A loving, committed marriage and family is a full expression of God's image.

Read through Genesis 1 again and underline every occurrence of the phrase "and God saw that *it was* good." What was God's observation of His completed project? (v. 31)

What do you think is involved in the word "good" as a description of Creation? Why might God have used this word about Creation rather than some other?

What would the "goodness" of God's creation have to do with the fact of His rest and the purpose of His rest on the seventh day of the week of Creation? (Gen. 2:1–3)

HUMANKIND'S PHYSICAL ENVIRONMENT

After surveying the grand sweep of the creation of the universe and all living things, Moses focuses in on the details of the creation of the first man and the first woman. Genesis 1:26–30 provides the theology of human creation. Genesis 2:4–25 gives us a tour of their home and a personal introduction. Let's look first at "Home, Sweet Home."

Notice the change in names for deity. What divine name appears consistently in Genesis 1:1—2:3? _____

This is a name of power. What divine name appears consistently in Genesis 2:4—3:24? _____

This compound name adds God's relational name to His name of power. Genesis 2:4—3:24 stresses God's intimate relationship with His human creatures.

Complete the chart below to show how Genesis 2:5, 6 parallels Genesis 1:2 in showing the need for divine intervention.

Gen. 1:2	Gen. 2:5, 6
The earth was without form, and void;	_____ _____ _____
and darkness *was* on the face of the deep.	_____ _____ _____
And the Spirit of God was hovering over the face of the waters.	_____ _____ _____

While Genesis 1:2 describes the earth before God worked on it as Creator, Genesis 2:5, 6 describes the earth before people worked on it as cultivators to populate and subdue it (1:28). Genesis 2:5, 6 describes the unpopulated earth, void of *cultivated* plant life, that existed on day six of Creation week before God made humans.

Answer the following questions from Genesis 2:7:

Where did the material part of man originate?

Where did the nonmaterial part of man originate?

Man is neither mineral or divine. What is he?

From Genesis 2:8–14, describe the home God made for the first man in each of the following aspects:

Its location

Its nature

Its ordinary occupants

Its special occupants

Its fertility

Its wealth

From Genesis 2:15–17, answer these questions about the Lord God's plans for man in the garden of Eden:

What were the man's tasks in the garden?

What might those roles have involved in a perfect environment?

Whom might the man have needed to guard against? (see also Gen. 3:1)

What was the positive command of the Lord God to the man about the garden?

What was the Lord God's prohibition to the man about the garden?

What were the promised consequences of disobeying this prohibition?

HUMANKIND'S SOCIAL ENVIRONMENT

The last part of Genesis 2 provides insight into the first man and the first woman. These sinless parents of the human race, handmade by God to bear His image, emerge as people with needs every reader can relate to.

As Adam went about his routines in the garden of Eden, what observation did the Lord God make about him? (Gen. 2:18)

What is the difference between being alone and being lonely?

In what sense was Adam alone when the Lord God was with him?

What was the Lord God's proposed solution to the aloneness of Adam? (Gen. 2:18)

WORD WEALTH

The Hebrew term translated "comparable to" does not mean "identical to" or even "similar to." It means "corresponding to." If you tear a one hundred dollar bill in half, the two pieces are not identical, but they belong together. The features on each halves are quite different but clearly related to a larger design than either depicts alone.

Along the edges that mark the torn sides, the two halves are most different and most corresponding because each of those edges complements every in and out of the other. In marriage male and female personalities, as well as bodies, are to correspond and complete one another in the same way. Franklin's image is on the one hundred dollar bill. God's is on the man and woman.

How did the Lord God reveal to Adam that in all of creation there was no "helper comparable to him"? (Gen. 2:19, 20)

What does Adam's ability to name all of the animals reveal about him?

WORD WEALTH

The Hebrew term *'ezer,* translated "helper" in Genesis 2:18 and 20, is not a synonym for servant or lowly assistant.

With one exception, all of the occurrences of *'ezer* refer to
help from God. Subservience is not in the word. The Lord
God created woman to be an agent of divine aid to complete
mankind and remove Adam's aloneness.

How does the manner in which the Lord God created
woman illustrate His plan to make a helper corresponding to
Adam? (Gen. 2:21, 22)

Although Adam provided the materials from which the
woman was made, he was completely passive during her creation. Why do you think God wanted it that way?

How does Adam's response to seeing the newly created
woman (Gen. 2:23) compare to his response to all of the other
creatures of the Lord God? (vv. 19, 20)

Similarities

Differences

In Genesis 2:24, what implications for marriage are contained in each of these clauses?

"A man shall leave his father and mother"

"A man shall . . . be joined to his wife"

"They shall become one flesh"

BIBLE EXTRA

Jesus based His main teaching about marriage on Genesis 2:24. See Matthew 19:4–6 and the parallel passage in Mark 10:5–9. The apostle Paul reasoned that this text teaches all husbands how to love their wives (Eph. 5:28–31) and all people to avoid sexual immorality (I Cor. 6:15–18).

To be naked before another is to be unprotected and vulnerable, exposed in every way. How is the statement "They were both naked . . . and were not ashamed" (Gen. 2:25) a vivid way of saying Adam and Eve were sinless people?

 FAITH ALIVE

What social needs can a pet provide for a person?

What social needs can a friend provide for a person that a pet cannot?

What social needs can a marriage partner provide for a person that a friend cannot?

How does the Creation account teach men and women to honor the other sex rather than their own?

Men

Women

Lesson 3/The Beginning of All Sin
(3:1—5:32)

A fan approached the aging Scottish poet and begged him for his autograph and a few lines of something original. The poet looked at the young woman for a few moments and took the album from her hands. He thought and then scrawled across the page,

"An original something, fair maid, you would win me
To write—but how shall I begin?
For I fear I have nothing original in me—
Excepting Original Sin."[1]

The poet made a pun on the word "original." The young autograph hound wanted an original composition, a few words put together in a fresh way, but the poet used the word "original" to refer to the beginning of something. There were no original words in him, in that sense, but there was original sin.

Original sin doesn't refer to the transgression of an imaginative offender who came up with one no one else had ever sinned before. Original sin refers to the first sin by the first sinners. Usually when theologians speak or write of original sin, they are interested in how the very first sin corrupts every descendant of the original sinners.

Is original sin's effect on humankind an inherited spiritual defect that makes people guilty before each of them commits his or her own sins? Or is the effect of original sin on the human race only an inherited weakness toward temptation, so that every person is spiritually innocent until he or she sins personally and earns his or her guilt?

Theological conclusions about humankind are difficult to reach, first of all, because there is so much information in the Bible. The second difficulty is that theological statements about humankind must give a satisfactory explanation of daily human experience. To begin to understand original sin, you have to begin with Genesis 3. What does Genesis say about how man and woman, created to showcase the image of God, became distorted pictures of goodness, fun-house mirror horrors that dishonor God and hurt one another?

THE APPEAL OF SIN

The first woman and the first man chose evil. They didn't stumble into sin because they were bored and had nothing better to do. For a moment, evil looked good and death looked like life itself, but then they experienced sin's betrayal just as their descendants have ever since.

Read Genesis 3 and underline every identification of the woman's tempter. How is he identified?

No further biblical identification of the tempter appears until the last book of the Bible, written some 1,500 years after Genesis. According to Revelation 12:9 and 20:2, who tempted the woman?

When the Lord God placed the man in the Garden of Eden, He told him, "Of every tree of the garden you may freely eat; but of the tree of the knowledge of good and evil you shall not eat, for in the day that you eat of it you shall surely die" (Gen. 2:16, 17).

How do you think the serpent wanted the woman to feel about this command of God when he asked his first leading question? (Gen. 3:1)

What does the response of the woman suggest about her thoughts concerning God's regulations about the trees of the garden? (Gen. 3:2, 3)

Why do you think the serpent denied that disobedience would bring the promised consequences? (Gen. 3:4)

What did the serpent say would happen if the woman disobeyed the command of the Lord God? (Gen. 3:5)

What did the serpent imply was the motive of the Lord God in prohibiting the man and woman from eating of the tree of the knowledge of good and evil?

The serpent never told the woman to eat the forbidden fruit. He deceived her (2 Cor. 11:3; 1 Tim. 2:14) so that she sinned without being directly told to. Based on Genesis 3:6, compare the sins of the woman and the man in the following aspects.

	THE WOMAN	THE MAN
Temptation:	_____	_____
Resistance:	_____	_____
	_____	_____
Motivation:	_____	_____
	_____	_____

"Through one man [Adam] sin entered the world" (Rom. 5:12). The man, not the woman, brought sin into the human race. Why is he the responsible party for rebelling against God?

THE CONSEQUENCES OF SIN

The serpent told the woman that the results of eating of the tree would be that she would "be like God, knowing good and evil" (Gen. 3:5). The actual results were far different. What was the first consequence of eating the fruit? (Gen. 3:7)

What did they do about this? (Gen. 3:7, 8)

What was the underlying motivation for concealing their nakedness? (Gen. 3:10)

Before sin, the man and the woman enjoyed an openness toward the Lord God and one another without shame or fear (Gen. 2:25). After sin, who did they instinctively defend themselves against in shame-filled fear?

In Genesis 3:8–10

In Genesis 3:11, 12

In Genesis 3:13

Since spiritual death is separation from God, how could the man and woman see evidence of their death in this first encounter with God after their sin?

Describe Adam's confession of his sin (Gen. 3:7–12):

In terms of his willingness to confess

In terms of the straightforwardness of his confession

How does the confession of the woman compare to that of the man? (Gen. 3:13)

Describe the Lord God's method of obtaining confessions from the man and the woman (Gen. 3:8–13):

In terms of His emotional reaction to sin

In terms of His emotional reaction to the sinners

In terms of His use of questions

In terms of what the sinners had to admit

Read through Genesis 3:14–19 and underline the occurrences of the word "cursed." On what or whom did the Lord God pronounce a curse?

Whom did the Lord God not curse as He pronounced the long-range consequences of sin on them?

What was the curse on the serpent? (Gen. 3:14–16)

BIBLE EXTRA

The Gospel's First Proclamation. [Genesis 3:15] contains the first proclamation of the gospel. All of the richness, the mercy, the sorrow, and the glory of God's redeeming work with man is here in miniature. God promises to bring a Redeemer from the Seed of the woman; He will be completely human yet divinely begotten. "That serpent of old, called the Devil," would war with the Seed (see Rev. 12) and would smite Him. But even as the Serpent struck at His heel, His foot would descend, crushing the Serpent's head.

In Christ's life and death this scripture was fulfilled. Divinely begotten, yet fully human, by His death and resurrection He has defeated and made a public spectacle of the powers of hell (Col. 2:15). This first messianic promise is one of the most succinct statements of the gospel to be found anywhere.[2]

What was the long-range consequence of the woman's sin? (Gen. 3:16)

What was the curse on the ground? (Gen. 3:17, 18)

How did the Lord God use the curse on the ground as the consequence of the man's sin? (Gen. 3:17–19)

Before the man and woman sinned, there had been perfect harmony in their relationship (Gen. 2:23–25). How would the long-range consequences of sin threaten the harmony of their marriage and every marriage after theirs? (Gen. 3:16–19)

How does the Lord God's clothing of Adam and Eve (Gen. 3:21) show His mercy on their sin-distorted lives? (see 2:25; 3:7–11)

How did the Lord God address His concern that Adam and Eve would use the tree of life to live forever physically? (Gen. 3:22–24)

In your opinion was it punishment or mercy on the Lord God's part to prevent Adam and Eve from living endlessly? Why?

  BIBLE EXTRA

Impact of the Fall. Through disobedience to the terms of his rule, man "falls," thus experiencing the loss of his "dominion" (Gen. 3:22, 23). Everything of his delegated realm (Earth) comes under a curse as his relationship with God, the fountainhead of his power to rule, is severed (vv. 17, 18). . . .

Through his disobedience to God and submission to the Serpent's suggestions, man's rule has been forfeited to the Serpent. . . . Amid the tragedy of this sequence of events, God begins to move redemptively, and a plan for recovering man's lost estate is promised (v. 15) and set in motion with the first sacrifice (v. 21).[3]

  FAITH ALIVE

How and why does sinful behavior cause you to withdraw from God and avoid contact with Him?

Who and/or what would you like to blame for the repeated sinful patterns of your life that are really difficult to gain victory over?

How does honest confession to the Lord God who forgives sins on the basis of the sacrifice of Jesus Christ help deal with broken fellowship and blame-shifting?

Depending on your gender, how have you participated in the long-range consequences of sin imposed on the human race at the time of Adam and Eve's sin? (Gen. 3:16, 17–19)

"For as by one man's [Adam's] disobedience many were made sinners, so also by one man's [Christ's] obedience many will be made righteous" (Rom. 5:19).

THE VIOLENCE OF SIN

The Lord God warned that sin would lead to immediate death (Gen. 2:17). The serpent scoffed at the Lord God as a cosmic killjoy and predicted that the woman would become like God if she had the nerve to disobey Him. Adam and Eve did sin, but they did not become like God. They died spiritually, and their offspring began spilling blood all over the earth. According to Genesis, violence is the visible symptom of the disease of sin.

What was the hope of Eve, reflected in her son's name, when Cain was born? (Gen. 4:1; see 3:15)

From the information in Genesis 4:2–5, compare the first two sons of Adam and Eve according to the following categories.

	CAIN	ABEL
Occupation	_____	_____
Sacrifice	_____	_____
Response of God	_____	_____
	_____	_____

From Genesis 4:5–10, analyze the sin of Cain according to the following aspects:

The emotional state that preceded it

God's proposal for eliminating the emotion

God's warning about the emotion

Cain's murder of his brother

Cain's response to God's invitation to confess (see Gen. 3:9–13)

Its special hideousness in God's eyes

Compare the consequences of Cain's sin with those of Adam's sin by means of the following chart.

SIN'S CONSEQUENCES

	ADAM Genesis 3:17–24	CAIN Genesis 4:11–15
Thing cursed		
Relation to the ground		
Response to punish-ment		
Divine protec-tion		
Expul-sion		

In his isolated exile "east of Eden" (Gen. 4:16), Cain fathered an energetic clan (vv. 17–22). What were some of the accomplishments of civilization first attributed in these verses to the descendants of Cain?

The fifth generation from Cain was Lamech. What were Lamech's contributions to the history of sin? (Gen. 4:19–24)

In marriage

In violence

In openness

In presuming on God's grace

How did God express His grace to bereaved Adam and Eve? (Gen. 4:25; 5:3)

 FAITH ALIVE

What makes anger such a difficult emotion with which to do anything constructive?

What makes you angry?

What is one thing that makes you angry to the point of violence?

How do you need to handle this temptation to violence with the help of God's grace?

THE UNIVERSALITY OF SIN

All of the descendants of Adam and Eve were sinners under the consequences the Lord God announced (Gen. 3:16–19) until the salvation He promised would occur (v. 15). Not all of humankind responded to sin and the Lord God the same way. Some embraced sin and revelled in selfish violence, and some embraced the Lord God in hope of deliverance.

What does Genesis 5:1–3 imply about humankind and the image of God after the entrance of sin into the human race? (James 1:9)

The descendants of Cain (Gen. 4:16–24) contrast sharply with the descendants of Seth (5:6–32). Who was the son of Cain?

Who was the son of Seth?

What "calling" did Cain's son engage in, and what did it mean? (4:17)

What "calling" did Seth's son engage in, and what did it mean? (v. 26)

Who was the fifth descendant from Cain, and what was he like?

Who was the fifth descendant from Seth, and what was he like?

Contrast these descendants of Cain and Seth who shared same name.

	CAIN'S FAMILY	SETH'S FAMILY
Enoch (4:17)	_____ (5:24)	_____
	_____	_____
Lamech (4:19–24)	_____ (5:28, 29)	_____
	_____	_____

Lamech was the seventh generation from Seth, but he was keenly aware of the curse on the ground because of human-kind's sin (Gen. 5:29; see 3:17–19). What does this reveal about the spiritual orientation of the descendants of Seth?

 FAITH ALIVE

All of the descendants of Adam's sons were separated from God by sin, but not all of them expressed the same degree of moral depravity. Why was this true?

What factors do you think affect how an unbeliever expresses his sin nature in his behavior?

What factors do you think influence how a born-again Christian expresses his sin nature in his behavior?

1. Thomas Campbell, "To a Young Lady, Who Asked Me to Write Something Original for Her Album."

2. *Spirit-Filled Life Bible* (Nashville, TN: Thomas Nelson Publishers, 1991), 9, "Kingdom Dynamics: The Gospel's First Proclamation."

3. Ibid., 10, 11, "Kingdom Dynamics: Impact of the Fall."

Lesson 4/The Beginning of All Judgment
(6:1—9:29)

George had never been in a federal courtroom before. The old courthouse was impressive enough with marble stairways and pillars, stained-glass windows, frescoed walls, and a soaring dome, but the courtroom proper was daunting. The floor-to-ceiling paneling looked like walnut, and the ceiling was a woodworker's dream. Around the chamber just below the ceiling, dictums about justice were carved in ornate moldings.

The group from George's church group was unusually subdued—more awed by the courtroom than the sanctuary at church. They were there in support of a Christian brother who had embezzled a significant amount of money from work and confessed when he was about to be exposed. That was nothing to be proud of, but when the moment came the brother had faced his guilt squarely before God, his employers, and his church. Now the trial was over and it was time for sentencing.

George and the others were there to reinforce an appeal for leniency that several had put in writing to the judge earlier. After a good deal of formal judicial ritual, the robed judge addressed the defendant. "The presence of so many community members in the courtroom today testifies to the esteem in which many hold you. I have read the appeals of many of these same individuals who have asked me to consider the punishment you have already endured in the loss of position and respect in your profession and civic standing. They have asked me to take into account the pain the sentence of this court will cause your family.

"And while this court is not insensitive to the losses you and your family are going through, this court will not be swayed by them. It is you, and not this court, who has inflicted these wounds on yourself and on your family. This court bears not a whit of responsibility for them.

"This court imposes the following penalties. . . ." But George was no longer listening to the details. His conscious mind had been overwhelmed by the stern majesty of unyielding justice. And when the scope of the sentence finally sank in, he wondered if the sentence of the judge wouldn't be easier to handle than the self-induced process of reaping what you sow. He felt sorry for his ashen-faced friend and tearful family.

THE CONDEMNED AND THE SPARED

All people have sinned, the Bible says, and no one naturally seeks after God as He really is (Rom. 3:11, 23). But God does work in the hearts of many people and moves them to desire Him. In the family of Adam's son Seth were many such people (Gen. 4:26; 5:24, 28, 29), but their presence was not enough to halt a world rushing toward judgment on wicked hearts and lives.

 BIBLE EXTRA

There are two major identifications of "the sons of God" and "the daughters of men" in Genesis 6:1–4. The view of the early church fathers was that "the sons of God" were angels who interbred with human women and by doing so incurred a special divine judgment. The expression "sons of God" usually refers to angels in the Old Testament (Job 1:6; 2:1). The passages about imprisoned angels in 1 Peter 3:19, 20; 2 Peter 2:4 and Jude 6 (all three verses precede references to the Flood) support this view.

The medieval view is that "the sons of God" and "daughters of men" are poetic references to the two branches of Adam's descendants in chapters 4 and 5. Once the godly line chose to intermarry with the godless line, the Lord's patience expired and He initiated the process of judgment.

The fallen angel view is linguistically superior, and better explains the Lord's disgust and anger over the inappropriateness of angels approaching women. The view about the two lines of the human race fits the preceding context better. It is also more consistent with the teaching of Jesus that angels do not (note, not "cannot," but "are not to") engage in sexual activity (Matt. 22:30).

Study the passage, check your commentaries, and confer with your pastor or Bible study leader about the position of your church on Genesis 6:1, 2.

What was the Lord's assessment of the spiritual condition of the human race before the Flood? (Gen. 6:5, 11, 12)

What was the Lord's emotional reaction to human degradation? (Gen. 6:6)

What did the Lord decide to do because of the wickedness of men and women? (Gen. 6:7, 13)

Why was the Lord's response to Noah different? (Gen. 6:8, 9)

 WORD WEALTH

"Noah found **grace** in the eyes of the LORD" (Gen. 6:8). The Hebrew term translated "grace" is usually translated "favor" in the Old Testament. Usually "favor" is not a theological concept but a social one involving people helping people. In addition, the focus is not on the giver of the favor but on the receiver. Noah had been prepared by the Lord God through his father and family traditions (Gen. 5:29) to receive God's favor.[1]

From Genesis 6:14–16, describe the ark in each of the following aspects:

Its construction materials

Its waterproofing

Its dimensions

Its openings

Its interior design

 WORD WEALTH

An **ark** was a "chest" or "box" for storage or shipping. Later in the tabernacle, the "ark of the covenant" was the special receptacle for storing the tablets on which the Lord wrote the Ten Commandments with His finger. Noah's vessel was called an "ark" rather than a ship because transportation was not its function. The "ark" God had Noah build was a receptacle for storing and preserving the people and the animals whom the Lord covenanted to save.

Why did God have Noah build the ark? (Gen. 6:17)

 WORD WEALTH

Genesis 6:18 contains the first use of the word **covenant** in the Bible. A "covenant" is a formal agreement or contract between two parties. Usually both parties commit themselves to doing something for their mutual benefit, but

often when God is involved He is the one who commits to action while people are the ones who benefit. In the covenant in Genesis 6, God pledged that He would deliver Noah's family and a sampling of all the animals. Noah's part was to build the ark (v. 22).

In Genesis 6:18–21, what were the terms of the covenant the Lord made with Noah in each of these areas?

People

Other creatures

Provisions

FAITH ALIVE

How have you experienced the activity of the Spirit of God in your life while striving against sin?

How have you received the Lord's favor in being spared judgment for your sins?

THE JUDGMENT ON HUMANKIND

Once the Lord determined that humanity had become so corrupt that He had to destroy it, the biblical narrative pays no more attention to the masses of people and animals that died in the judgment. By contrast, Genesis 7 and 8 give a detailed account of the deliverance from judgment of Noah's family and the representative group of animals.

In Genesis 7:2, 3 the Lord gave more detailed instructions to Noah about animals for the ark. How many of each of the following was Noah to take on the ark?

Clean animals

Unclean animals

Birds

Why did the Lord have Noah take more clean animals and birds than unclean animals? (Gen. 8:20)

Where did the waters come from that flooded the earth in judgment? (Gen. 7:11)

How did the Flood accomplish its terrible work of judgment? (Gen. 7:20–24)

What actions did the Lord take relative to the salvation of man and beasts in each of these passages from Genesis?

6:20

7:1–4

7:16

8:1–3

8:15–17

WORD WEALTH

"'But God remembered Noah' (8:1). Just when all seemed lost, God paid attention to Noah and lavished his loving care on him — for that is what the verb 'remember' means in Scripture. To remember in the biblical sense of that term is not merely to recall to mind or to refresh one's memory. To remember someone means to express concern for him, to visit him with gracious love."[2]

FAITH ALIVE

How have you seen the Lord judge sin in your life or in the life of someone else? Did He allow sowing and reaping to take its course, or did He intervene directly?

How was the judgment you described above an act of mercy and preservation for the one judged or for others?

A FRESH START FOR MANKIND

When the eight members of Noah's family and the army of animals finally stood outside the ark—the only living creatures on the entire planet—it was time for a new beginning.

This beginning could not be like the one in Eden because of the presence of sin, so God needed to tell Noah the ground rules for this fresh start.

Describe Noah's sacrifice to the Lord after the Flood. How long do you think it took him to complete this sacrifice? What do you think it meant to Noah? (Gen. 8:20)

According to Genesis 8:21, 22, what was the Lord's response to the burnt offering by Noah in each of these areas?

Noah's worship

God's negative promise

God's positive promise (even though worded negatively)

God gave instructions to Noah and his sons in their new world that are reminiscent of the instructions He gave to Adam in the garden. Compare Genesis 9:1, 2 with 1:28–30. Point out the similarities and differences in the following areas:

Blessing

Relationship to other animals

Food

Compare God's commands in Genesis 9:5, 6 with Cain's sin in 4:8–15. Point out the cause-effect relationship in these areas.

Regulation of murder

Significance of blood in murder

Consequences of murder

Although humankind's environment had been totally remade, what does the explicit commandment concerning murder reveal about the nature of human hearts?

In Genesis 6:18 the Lord had covenanted to preserve Noah's family and representative animals. In Genesis 9:8–17 the Lord made another covenant of preservation. Describe this covenant the Lord made with the survivors of the Flood in each of these areas:

Parties to the covenant

Promise of the covenant

Sign of the covenant

Function of the sign

BIBLE EXTRA

After the Flood. The Flood has not reversed the loss of man's original dominion. He is still fallen, though thankfully a recipient of God's mercy. Further, the animals will fear mankind from this time on (9:2), which was not characteristic of their relationship prior to this. In the ultimate restoration of God's kingdom on Earth, the original fearless order will be regained (Is. 11:6–9).

Notwithstanding these deficiencies, a cleansed realm for seeking God's kingdom first is newly available to man. . . . The Flood has not neutralized the influence of the Serpent, nor has it changed mankind's capacity for rebellion against God's rule. Nevertheless, new hope dawns with promise for the eventual recovery of what was lost of his first estate.[3]

FAITH ALIVE

What fresh starts has the Lord granted you in your life?

How have you thanked Him?

If you were going to plan a special time of thanksgiving to God for all of the fresh starts He has given you for eternity and for this life, what would you do?

Why not do it?

THE REAPPEARANCE OF SIN AND CONSEQUENCES

Human sinfulness soon reasserted itself in the new society after the Flood. The Israelites to whom Moses wrote Genesis would have found the story of renewed sinfulness very interesting as they prepared to conquer the land of Canaan.

Who were the sons of Noah? (Gen. 9:18)

What was their significance for the post-diluvian world? (Gen. 9:19)

What occupation did Noah follow after the Flood? (Gen. 9:20)

From Genesis 9:21–27, describe the emerging decadence in part of Noah's family.

Noah's folly

The action of Ham compared to the action of Shem and Japheth

The attitude of Ham compared to the attitude of Shem and Japheth

Noah's response to what Ham did

What may be implied about Canaan's character

Noah's response to Shem (ancestor of Israel) and Japheth

 BEHIND THE SCENES

The descendants of Ham's son Canaan inhabited the land which the Lord would promise to Abraham, Isaac, and Jacob. The patriarchs lived in the land of Canaan as strangers and pilgrims, but the Lord assigned the nation Moses led out of Egypt the task of driving the Canaanites out and occupying the land as their own.

Clearly this portion of the Genesis account is intended to show the early beginnings of the spirit of Canaanitish corruption in Canaan, their forefather. The "prophetic curse" establishes an early point of understanding for the future judgment eventually to be visited in Joshua's time. Of the Canaanites the Lord said, "The land is defiled; therefore I visit the punishment of its iniquity upon it, and the land vomits out its inhabitants" (Lev. 18:25). Read Leviticus 18, which warns Israel against behaving like the descendants of Canaan. Twenty-four times in that chapter the Lord prohibits various sinful ways of "uncovering nakedness."

1. Edwin Yamauchi, "Hen," *Theological Wordbook of the Old Testament,* Vol. I (Chicago, IL: Moody Press, 1980), 694.

2. Ronald F. Youngblood, *The Book of Genesis: An Introductory Commentary* (second edition; Grand Rapids, MI: Baker Book House, 1991), 101.

3. *Spirit-Filled Life Bible* (Nashville, TN: Thomas Nelson Publishers, 1991), 18, "Kingdom Dynamics: After the Flood."

Lesson 5/The Beginning of All Nations
(10:1—11:32)

Mike's dad knew all the family stories. When the extended family gathered for holidays at grandmother's house, Mike's dad could be counted on to tell at least one story about a distant relative, long dead, whose life had some bearing on the grown-ups' conversation in the living room.

Mike couldn't imagine how his dad knew all that stuff, but he could talk for hours with enthusiasm about ancestors on the farflung limbs of the family tree as though those people were his dearest friends. Mike knew his dad maintained an ancient scrapbook that his mother had started decades ago. On rare occasions his dad pored over those yellowing pages, but mostly he practiced the art of passing it on.

Mike had always noticed that dad told stories that he had heard from older family members, and that he told them the same way every time. Somehow to his dad these stories were the family, and these stories were the land. Each person lived up a hollow or down a creek, near a store, mill, schoolhouse, or church.

Every story assumed that each listener envisioned the bearded men, bonneted women, and barefoot children in their places. Mike noticed as a child that his grandparents, aunts, and uncles nodded along with his dad and added bits to the tales. But Mike and his cousins didn't live in those hills. Many of the stories might as well have happened in Tibet or Timbuktu as far as they were concerned.

When he was little, Mike assumed that one day he would know all the stories his dad knew and that the family would listen to him. Later he didn't want to know the stories, but later still he felt sad and more than a little lonely for all of those forebears who would always be strangers to him but who had been such good company for his dad.

What a loss to us all, Mike had thought. One day it dawned on him that his younger sister knew a lot of the stories, and he knew that it hadn't been his place to remember them. It was hers. She simply did it.

THE DESCENDANTS OF NOAH

When Moses wrote the Book of Genesis for the Israelites who had just left Egypt to begin life as a nation in the land of Canaan, he wanted them to know the stories that defined them. The story of Noah's family was a crucial one because all nations of the earth descended from his three sons. If Israel was to understand the background of their ancestor Abraham, their Egyptian slavemasters, and the wicked Canaanites who awaited them in the Promised Land, they needed to know about Noah's sons.

Who were Noah's three sons, and what order do their names appear in when they are listed together? (Gen. 5:32; 6:9; 9:18; 10:1)

This repeated order is their order of importance in Old Testament history. Few of Japheth's descendants figure in the Old Testament, so he is listed last. Later you will observe why Shem always comes first. Look up the biblical clues about who was oldest and who was youngest so you can arrange Noah's sons in their birth order.

Oldest (Gen. 10:21)

Middle (Who's left?)

Youngest (Gen. 9:24)

From the genealogy in Genesis 10, list the sons of Shem, Ham, and Japheth in the family tree below.

Noah
|

Japheth   Shem   Ham
| | |

_____ _____ _____

_____ _____ _____

_____ _____ _____

_____ _____ _____

_____ _____

_____

_____

Which families figured prominently in the interests of the Israelites wandering in the wilderness to whom Moses wrote Genesis?

From which family did Abram (Abraham) come? (Gen. 10:24, 25; 11:10–26)

Which family had enslaved them in Egypt? (Gen. 10:6, 13, 14)

Which family would they dispossess from the Promised Land? (Gen. 10:6, 15–19)

How is Shem identified in Genesis 10:21?

(Eber is the person whose name probably is the source of the word "Hebrew," a shorthand way of saying "son of Eber." This is why Shem is always listed first among the sons of Noah. Ham is listed next because his descendants would oppose the descendants of Shem.)

FAITH ALIVE

Of what personal comfort should it be to you to know that God has kept track of these people in Genesis 10 when secular history easily dismissed them from memory as insignificant?

What importance do these genealogies suggest there is in passing on to the next generation a fear and reverence for the Lord?

THE SCATTERING OF THE NATIONS

The genealogies of Genesis 10 do not explain how the descendants of Noah came to scatter. There is a hint bound up in the name Peleg (vv. 25, 32) that begs for an explanation. What is that hint?

What uniting characteristic of humankind after the Flood did Moses highlight for his readers? (Gen. 11:1)

Where did the united descendants of Noah's sons finally settle as they migrated together away from where the ark had deposited them? (Gen. 11:2)

Look up Daniel 1:1, 2 for the more usual biblical name for this area.

What ancient hero is associated with this area? (Gen. 10:8–10)

What accomplishment is credited to him by the lists of Genesis 10:10–12?

What plan of action did the descendants of Noah's sons counsel among themselves to take? (Gen. 11:4a)

What building materials were available to them? (Gen. 11:3)

With what corresponding building materials were Moses' readers familiar?

What were the goals of this building project? (Gen. 11:4b)

Positively

Negatively

How did the goals of Noah's descendants conflict with the goals assigned them by the Lord? (Gen. 9:1, see 1:28)

BEHIND THE SCENES

> Genesis 11:5 doesn't mean that the Lord was unaware of what the united population of the earth was doing until He happened to make a personal inspection tour. Genesis 11:5 is a turning point in this account like 9:1 is the turning point in the Flood narrative. Genesis 9:1 doesn't imply that the Lord had forgotten Noah's family and the animals. These turning point verses both mean that when the time was exactly right, the Lord got actively involved in the flow of events.

What did the Lord observe was troublesome about the unity of the human race? (Gen. 11:6)

Why was it a bad idea for humankind to achieve all of its purposes? (Gen. 11:6)

What did the Lord counsel within Himself to do? (Gen. 11:7; see 1:26 for a similar counsel)

What were the results of the confusion of languages within the descendants of Noah? (Gen. 11:8, 9)

For the people

For the city and tower

Why was the confusion of the languages an effective way for scattering people over a wide geographical area?

What did the incomplete city and tower come to represent?

BEHIND THE SCENES

Babel is derived from the Hebrew *balal,* which means "mixed up" or "confused." The Babylonians later interpreted "Babel" to mean "the gate of the god." Most scholars link this city with Babylon, which eventually became the fountainhead of all demon worship and finally, in Revelation, becomes synonymous with the final evil city that deifies evil and persecutes God's people (Rev. 17 and 18).[1]

FAITH ALIVE

What are the implications of the Tower of Babel account for the origin of and basis for the sin of racism? How did the attitude that prompted the building of the tower turn into hatred and suspicion?

What does the Lord have to do in the hearts and minds of born-again men and women to sanctify them from racist attitudes?

FROM SHEM TO ABRAM

To illustrate the division of the nations that occurred during the lifetime of Peleg (Gen. 10:25), Moses repeated the genealogy of Shem in Genesis 11, but he diverged from the one given in chapter 10 after the generation that was at Babel. Fill in the following blanks with the names of successive generations in the family tree of Shem based on the lists in Genesis 10:22–29 and 11:10–26.

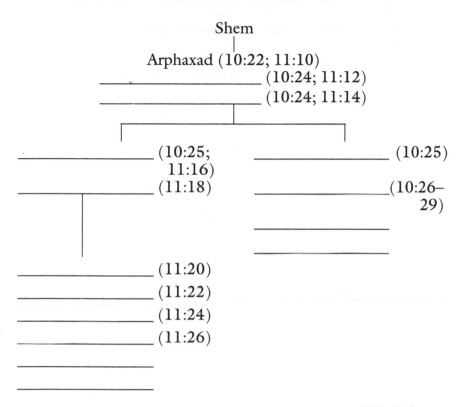

From Genesis 11:27–29, answer the following questions about Terah's family:

Where was Terah's home?

What were the names of Terah's sons?

Which one died before his father?

Which child of Haran figures most prominently in Genesis? (v. 27; see 12:4)

Who were Haran's other children? (v. 29)

Who was Nahor's wife, and what was her connection to Terah's family?

Who was Abram's wife, and what was her connection to Terah's family? (see Gen. 20:12)

Whom did Terah take with him when he left Ur? (Gen. 11:31)

Why did he leave Ur?

How far did he get before he settled down?

Terah journeyed a long way when he moved from Ur of the Chaldeans to Haran in upper Mesopotamia, but when he settled there Terah was still a long way from his destination in the land of Canaan. It would be up to his son Abram to complete the odyssey for different reasons than those of Terah's.

According to Joshua 24:2, what was the religious orientation of the family of Abram?

When did Abram, the son of a pagan, first hear the call of God? (Acts 7:2–4)

 BEHIND THE SCENES

"Joshua 24:2 shows that Terah and his forbears 'served other gods'; his own name and those of Laban, Sarah and

Milcah point towards the moon-god as perhaps the most prominent of these. Certainly Ur and Haran were centres of moon worship, which may suggest why the migration halted when it did. Terah's motives in leaving Ur may have been no more than prudence (the Elamites destroyed the city c. 1950 B.C.); but Abram had already heard the call of God."[2]

 ## FAITH ALIVE

How far back in your family history have your ancestors been born-again believers in the Lord Jesus? (If it's farther back than you know, how many generations that you know about have served the Lord?)

Has anyone in your family made choices because of their faith that have affected their occupation, place of residence, or other major aspect of life? If so, what happened?

How have extended family members been affected by the step of faith you wrote about in the previous question?

1. *Spirit-Filled Life Bible* (Nashville, TN: Thomas Nelson Publishers, 1991), 21, note on Genesis 11:9.

2. Taken from *Genesis* (TOTC) by Derek Kidner. © 1967 by Tyndale Press. Used by permission of InterVarsity Press, P.O. Box 1400, Downers Grove, IL 60515.

Lesson 6/The Promise of a New Beginning
(12:1—14:24)

It was movie day in science class in the fall of 1957. The lights went out, the projector whirred and clattered in the back of the room, and dust motes drifted through the beam of light as it expanded to fill the screen with a flickering black-and-white image that jerked and swallowed a word at every splice. Every kid in the room felt like he or she was getting away with something. The teacher acted like this was part of school, but they knew better.

On the screen, the neatly groomed actor-playing-scientist wore a crisp white lab coat as he smiled at the one camera and patiently explained how every atom of uranium was a little solar system with electrons orbiting its nucleus as the planets orbited the sun. Scientists could shoot a nuclear bullet called an alpha particle from a nuclear gun called a cyclotron and hit the nucleus of an atom of uranium.

The talking head on the screen said that the nucleus would split, emitting lots of energy and another alpha particle bullet streaking off to shatter another uranium atom. In no time miniature uranium solar systems would be exploding all over the place in a chain reaction. A controlled chain reaction generates usable energy and an uncontrolled chain reaction is an atom bomb.

Did he say atom bomb! Every twelve-year-old boy in the audience wondered if he had the right stuff in the basement to make one of those babies. Several mushroom clouds blossomed over the school in imaginations around the room.

But the movie was just getting good. Finally the scientist held up the ping pong ball he had been fingering all the while he droned on about holocausts on uranium worlds. "This ball represents an alpha particle," he said. As he turned away, the camera panned to an elevated surface that stretched away into the darkness.

Everyone in the classroom sat up straight and stared at the screen. The surface was covered with hundreds of mouse-traps! Each trap was set, and a ping pong ball balanced on the wire bail ready to be hurled into the air if the trap were triggered.

"Each trap represents an atom of uranium," Mr. Scientist continued. "Watch the chain reaction that is triggered by just one nuclear bullet fired into a large enough mass of uranium." And he tossed his ping pong ball onto the bed of mousetraps. One ball sprang up, then several, and the table top exploded like popcorn into a field of bouncing ping pong balls.

The science movie ended, and the window shades went up. Many faces still wore a look that said, "Wow! One ping pong ball could start all that!"

THE CALL AND PREPARATION OF ABRAM

The rest of the Bible after Genesis 12 records the spiritual chain reaction set in motion by God when He called Abram to leave Ur of the Chaldeans and by faith enter a covenant relationship with Him. How could such an inauspicious beginning in the household of a pagan named Terah have such far-reaching consequences?

From Genesis 12:1–3, describe the call of God to Abram in these areas.

A break with the past

Personal benefits

Implications for other people

BIBLE EXTRA

God's Heart to Prosper His People. In this passage God promises to make Abraham great; and God did bless Abraham in many ways, including material blessings. . . . The dynamic of this historic fact becomes pertinent to every believer today.

In Galatians 3:13, 14, God promises to give all believers the blessings of Abraham, telling us that Jesus became a curse for us so that we might receive "the blessings of Abraham." This begins, of course, with our being born again, or becoming new creatures in Christ Jesus.

But "the blessings of Abraham" involve other things as well. The Lord wants us to prosper—spiritually, emotionally and physically, and materially. The blessings are ours by His promise, and we need make no apology for the fact that prosperity is included.[1]

AT A GLANCE

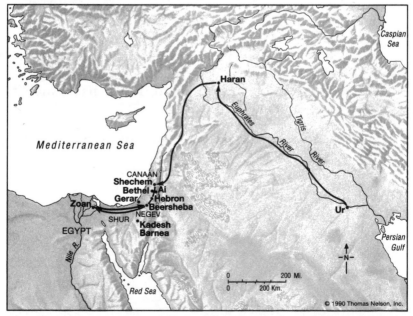

Abraham's 1,500-mile journey was fueled by faith. See Hebrews 11:8–10.[2]

From Genesis 12:4–9, describe Abraham's journey in obedience to the call of the Lord.

Place of departure

Destination

Fellow travelers

First stop in the new land

First encounter with the Lord in the new land

Second stop and encounter with the Lord in the new land

General course of Abram's movements in the new land

 BEHIND THE SCENES

Shechem and **Bethel** became important locations in the Promised Land for the descendants of Abraham. Later Jacob would come to these same two places after he had lived in Haran for some time (Gen. 33:18; 35:1).

Bethel was the place where the Lord first made His covenant with Jacob (Gen. 28:10–22). "Shechem . . . was marked out as a place of decision. Here the Israelites would be assembled to choose between blessing and cursing (Dt. 11:29, 30), here Joshua would give his last charge (Jos. 24), and here the kingdom of Solomon would one day break in two (I Ki. 12)."[3]

From Genesis 12:10–20, describe how the Lord protected His newly chosen servant from the Pharaoh of Egypt, perhaps the most powerful man on earth at the time.

Reason Abram went to Egypt

Scheme to protect his life in a strange land

How the scheme worked

How the Lord protected Sarai and Abram

Pharaoh's response to the intervention of the Lord

FAITH ALIVE

How has the Lord singled you out from everyone else? What do you sense that He has uniquely for you to do in serving Him?

Who is the Lord blessing through their association with you like He blessed Lot through his association with Abram?

How have you recently experienced the protection of the Lord as one of His chosen people?

THE SEPARATED AND THE COMPROMISED

Abram's nephew Lot experienced blessing because of his association with Abram, but Lot did not share Abram's commitment to the call of the Lord. Lot is emphasized in Genesis to help readers understand by contrast what was special about Abram's relationship with God.

According to Genesis 13:1–4, how did Abraham retrace his steps when leaving Egypt? (see 12:8–10)

Geographically

Spiritually

Describe the conflict that arose between the households of Abram and Lot. (Gen. 13:2, 5–7)

How did the presence of the Canaanites and Perizzites all around make the conflict between Abram and Lot more dangerous? (Gen. 13:7)

From Genesis 13:8, 9, describe Abram's solution to his conflict with Lot.

Basis for resolution

Method of resolution

From Genesis 13:10–13, describe Lot's response to Abram's conflict resolution in these areas:

The advantages he saw

The disadvantages he overlooked

At Bethel, Abram "called on the name of the LORD" (Gen. 13:4) and then graciously and sacrificially resolved a dispute with Lot. How did the Lord respond to Abram? (Gen. 13:14–17)

In terms of territory

In terms of descendants

From Genesis 13, contrast Abram and Lot in each of these areas:

Fundamental value

Selflessness

What territory they ended up with

Where they ended up

BEHIND THE SCENES

Hebron served as the center for Abram's life and activity in the land of Canaan. Eventually he bought property here for the family burial site (Gen. 23), the only part of the Promised Land he ever owned. The nomadic lives of Abraham, Isaac, and Jacob, who all owned vast herds of livestock, were best suited to the open semiarid grasslands south of Hebron.

FAITH ALIVE

In Genesis 13 Abram and Lot illustrate the teaching of Jesus: "Whoever desires to save his life will lose it, but whoever loses his life for My sake will find it" (Matt. 16:25). How have you seen this truth illustrated in your experience?

How does closeness to God (see Gen. 13:4, 18) make sacrificial generosity more natural and attractive?

How does selfishness make closeness to the world more natural and attractive?

THE STRENGTH OF RIGHTEOUSNESS

Lot thought he was smart in choosing "all the plain of Jordan" as his dwelling (Gen. 13:10). He thought he would end up richer and more powerful than Uncle Abram. For the first time (but not the last) Uncle Abram had to rescue Lot. Lot seemed unable to see that Abram's spiritually motivated choices had led to greater power than his materially motivated ones had.

BEHIND THE SCENES

Four kings from the east and north attacked five kings of the southern Jordan valley where Lot had chosen to live in an effort to get rich. Ironically, three of the invading kings—Amraphel, Arioch, and Chedorlaomer—came from Shinar and neighboring territories which Lot had abandoned years previously with his uncle and grandfather (Gen. 11:31, 32). The fourth king, Tidal, may have been a Hittite from Asia Minor.

The five cities of Sodom, Gomorrah, Admah, Zeboiim, and Zoar were clustered at the southern end of the Dead Sea, called Siddim and the Salt Sea in Genesis 14. Sodom apparently was the leading city of the five, Gomorrah second, while Zoar was the smallest of the five (Gen. 19:20, 22). Admah and Zeboiim were close enough to Sodom and Gomorrah geographically and morally to share in their eventual destruction by God (Gen. 10:19; Deut. 29:23; Hos. 11:8).

Why did the four kings from the east and north invade the land of Canaan in the days when Lot lived in the vicinity of Sodom? (Gen. 14:4)

BEHIND THE SCENES

The rebellion involved more cities and their petty kings than the five cities of Siddim. Following the caravan routes from north to south, the invading armies of the four kings initially bypassed the cities of Siddim in order to deal with four rebel groups in extreme southern Canaan (Gen. 14:5, 6). Then they turned back to the north and conquered two more rebel peoples near Kadesh Barnea (v. 7). That left the five kings of Siddim to mop up before going home.

How did the battle begin between the invading armies of the four kings and the defending armies of the cities of Siddim? (Gen. 14:8, 9)

BEHIND THE SCENES

Genesis 14:10 describes the area around the five cities of Siddim. The site of this battle, as well as those of Sodom, Gomorrah, Admah, and Zeboiim, was covered by the Dead Sea after the divine judgment on the wicked cities in Genesis 19. The Hebrew of Genesis 14:10 could be translated, " 'Now the Valley of Siddim was one bitumen pit after another.' The Dead Sea region is rich in minerals, and the sea was known in Roman times as *Asphaltites,* from the lumps of bitumen often found floating on its surface, especially in the southern area. These can be quite massive objects."[4]

What was the military outcome of the battle between the four invading kings and the five defending kings? (Gen. 14:10, 11)

What was the biblically important outcome of this battle that caused the Lord to include all the detail that is part of the first 11 verses? (Gen. 14:12)

From Genesis 14:13–17, describe Abram's rescue of Lot.

Abram's base of operations (also see Gen. 13:18)

Abram's intelligence source

Abram's allies (see v. 24)

Abram's fighting force

Abram's strategy of attack

Abram's success

Who was Melchizedek? (Gen. 14:18; see Heb. 7:1, 2) (Salem would later bear the expanded name *Jerusalem.*)

WORD WEALTH

Most High translates the Hebrew adjective *'elyon,* which means "uppermost, supreme, lofty, exalted, elevated." *'Elyon* is derived from *'alah* meaning "to ascend." [Do you notice the similarity to this term of the Arabic word for God?] *'Elyon* appears as an adjective more than 20 times, describing exalted rulers and even the highest rooms in the wall of the temple (Ezek. 41:7).

It becomes a divine title when paired with another name of God, such as *'El 'Elyon* or *'Elohim 'Elyon,* "God Most High." Compare the angels' declaration at the birth of Jesus: "Glory to God in the **highest,** and on earth peace, goodwill toward men!" (Luke 2:14).[5]

How do Melchizedek's actions and words explain why Abram succeeded where eleven armies (Gen. 14:5–10) had failed? (vv. 18–20)

How do Abram's responses to Melchizedek and the king of Sodom further explain why he succeeded where eleven armies had failed? (Gen. 14:20–24)

FAITH ALIVE

How have you seen faith in the Lord accomplish things that human effort and power could not?

What do you think is the relationship between faith in God and refusal to be allied closely with wicked people?

1. *Spirit-Filled Life Bible* (Nashville, TN: Thomas Nelson Publishers, 1991), 22, "Kingdom Dynamics: God's Heart to Prosper His People."

2. Ibid., map on 23.

3. Taken from *Genesis* (TOTC) by Derek Kidner. © 1967 by Tyndale Press. Used by permission of InterVarsity Press, P.O. Box 1400, Downers Grove, IL 60515.

4. Ibid.

5. *Spirit-Filled Life Bible*, 26, "Word Wealth: 14:18 Most High."

Lesson 7/ The Promise of a New People
(15:1—20:18)

Ten years had passed since the Lord had brought Abram to Canaan (Gen. 16:3) and promised to give it to him and to his numerous descendants (12:2; 13:16). Abram and Sarai began to experience some real doubts about whether God's plan was going to work out.

Based on the events of Genesis 14, what did the Lord mean when he told Abram the following in Genesis 15:1?

"Do not be afraid, Abram. I *am* your shield."

"Do not be afraid, Abram. I *am* . . . your exceedingly great reward."

Abram wasn't afraid of armies, but he did have a fear. What was it? (Gen. 15:3, 4)

BEHIND THE SCENES

Archaeologists have unearthed documents from the second millennium B.C. that "illustrate the fact that if a man did not have a son of his own, he could legally adopt a young man and pass his inheritance on to his newly adopted son.

Often the adopted son would be one of the man's servants, a servant he had come to know and trust, a servant who had perhaps already demonstrated his dependability around the household in a variety of ways."[1]

How did the Lord address Abram's fear? (Gen. 15:4, 5)

What was Abram's response to the Lord's promise? (Gen. 15:6)

 WORD WEALTH

Accounted translates the Hebrew verb *chashab,* which means "to think, reckon, calculate, imagine, to put one's thoughts together." *Chashab* is the consideration of a great number of elements, which results in a conclusion based on a wide overview. In this verse, God added up everything that Abram's belief meant to Him, and computing it all together, determined that it was equal to righteousness [see Rom. 4:1–3].[2]

From Genesis 15:7–21, describe each of these aspects of the covenant God made with Abram:

Its relationship to Abram's faith

The offerings of the covenant ceremony

Promises of the covenant

Abram's role in the ceremony

The Lord's role in the ceremony (represented by the oven and torch)

From Genesis 16:1–15, describe Sarai's plan to get a son by means of her Egyptian maid Hagar by explaining the following:

Her response to her fear (Gen. 16:1–4a)

Her response to the success of her scheme (Gen. 16:4b–6)

The Lord's protection of Abram's unborn child (Gen. 16:7–9)

The revelation by the angel to Hagar (Gen. 16:10–12)

Hagar's action in response to revelation (Gen. 16:13–15)

 FAITH ALIVE

For what problem in your life that has seemed to drag on for a long time do you have trouble trusting the Lord to handle according to His Word?

What have you done to handle this problem in order to "help the Lord along"?

What is to be gained in your situation by waiting on the Lord and lost by hurrying Him along?

THE SIGN AND CERTAINTY OF THE PROMISE

The Lord did not get flustered by Abram and Sarai's attempts to do His work for Him by bringing Ishmael into the world. He assured them both that His covenant would be fulfilled in His way, in His own time. The responses of Abram and Sarai to the Lord's assurances sound uncomfortably contemporary.

Trace the aging of Abram in the following passages:

	AGE	EVENT
Gen. 12:4	_____	_____
		_____
Gen. 16:16	_____	_____
		_____
Gen. 17:1	_____	_____
		_____

In Genesis 17:1, 2 the Lord summarized both sides of the covenant He was preparing to repeat and expand. What was Abram's part?

What was God's part?

For this expression of the Lord's covenant with Abram, everyone involved was given a new name. Complete the chart of new names and their meanings.

	NAME	MEANING
Gen. 17:1	_____	*El Shaddai* emphasizes God's might over against the frailty of man.[3]
Gen. 17:5	_____	_____
Gen. 17:15	_____	Princess

BIBLE EXTRA

The Words We Speak. . . . In this text [Gen. 17:5] God changes Abram's name to Abraham and promises Abraham that he will become the father of many nations. "Abram" means "High Father" or "Patriarch." "Abraham" means "Father of a Multitude." Thus, God was arranging that every time Abraham heard or spoke his own name, he would be reminded of God's promise. . . .

The principle: Let God's words, which designated His will and promise for *your* life, become as fixed in your mind and as governing of your speech as God's changing Abraham's name was in shaping his concept of himself. Do not "name" yourself anything less than God does.[4]

As an expansion of the covenant summary of Genesis 17:2, what did Almighty God promise to do in each of these verses?

17:6

17:7

17:8

As an expansion of the covenant summary of Genesis 17:2, what did Almighty God require of Abraham in each of these passages?

17:9

17:10, 11

17:12, 13

17:14

From Genesis 17:15–22, comment on the exchange between God and Abraham about a son for Abraham.

God Almighty's promise about Sarah

Abraham's counter-proposal to God's promise

God Almighty's final word about Ishmael

God Almighty's final word about Isaac

How did Abraham respond to the expanded covenant with God Almighty? (Gen. 17:23–27)

How did the Lord appear on another occasion to Abraham? (Gen. 18:1, 2, 22, 33; 19:1)

How did Abraham treat his anonymous guests? (Gen. 18:3–8)

What was new about this promise of a son to Abraham and Sarah? (Gen. 18:9, 10)

Compare and contrast Abraham and Sarah's reactions to God's promise of a son.

Compare 17:17 and 18:12a

Contrast 17:18 and 18:12b

Contrast 17:17a and 18:15

What was the Lord's answer to Sarah's doubts? (Gen. 18:14)

FAITH ALIVE

What makes the difference between a doubt like Abraham's (Gen. 17:17) that drives a person to the Lord and a doubt like Sarah's (18:12, 15) that pulls a person away from Him?

What things in your life have confirmed that nothing is "too hard for the LORD"?

THE MISERY OF THE COMPROMISER

While God was confirming to Abraham and Sarah that the time was ripe for the next generation of the people of promise to be born, the time was also ripe for the birth of the last generation of people of perversion in Sodom and Gomorrah. Ironically, Lot, who had come to Canaan in association with the people of promise, now was identified with the people of perversion.

Why did the Lord inform Abraham fully about His plans to destroy Sodom and Gomorrah? (Gen. 18:16–19)

Why was the Lord personally visiting Sodom and Gomorrah? (Gen. 18:20, 21)

Why did Abraham intervene on behalf of Sodom and Gomorrah? (Gen. 18:22, 23; see 14:14)

In Genesis 18:23–32, Abraham interceded with the Lord on behalf on any righteous people in Sodom and Gomorrah. What is revealed about his praying in the following areas?

Compassion

Breadth of his concern

Justice

Boldness

Tenacity

Faith

Partnership with God in His work

BIBLE EXTRA

At least three important principles emerge from God's conversation with Abraham in chapter 18. 1) We learn that wicked Sodom could have been spared for the sake of only 10 righteous people. From this we learn that it is not the presence of evil that brings God's mercy and long-suffering to an end; rather it is the absence of good! 2) Although God sometimes inspires us to pray by showing us things to come (v. 17), our intercession must be in line with God's character and covenant with men. Like Abraham, we may appeal to God to preserve His name, honor, and perfect justice before the world (v. 25). 3) Although we often measure influence by numbers, man's arithmetic cannot be used to estimate the impact of the righteous. God saves by many or by few.[5]

How did Lot's actions as a host (Gen. 19:1–3) compare with Abraham's? (18:1–8)

What does the confrontation between Lot and the citizens of Sodom in Genesis 19:4–9 reveal?

About the depravity of Sodom

About the courage of Lot

About the morality of Lot

About Lot's influence in Sodom

About the danger Lot was in

About the number of righteous people in Sodom

From Genesis 19:10–30, describe Lot's experiences during the judgment of Sodom.

His rescue from the Sodomites

Lot's attempt to rescue others from Sodom

Lot's attitude toward the judgment on Sodom

Apparent attitude of Lot's wife toward the judgment

Effect of judgment on Lot's emotions and spirit

Contrast the view Abraham saw in Genesis 19:27, 28 with the one Lot had seen in Genesis 13:10.

What impact had the immorality of Sodom had on the daughters of Lot? (Gen. 19:31–36)

What was the result of the incestuous relationship of Lot and his daughters? (Gen. 19:36–38)

Contrast what Lot had hoped to gain by choosing to move to Sodom (Gen. 13:10) with what he ended up with. (Gen. 19:30–38)

THE PRESERVATION OF SARAH

Before "the son of promise" was born, the Lord had to preserve "the mother of promise." Man of faith that Abraham was, he still had some bad habits—customs picked up, perhaps, from his pagan father—that got him into trouble. In the opening verses of Genesis 20, Abraham and Sarah make a journey. Where was their starting point? (Gen. 13:18; 18:1)

Where did they end up? (20:1)

See the map in Lesson 6, page 66, for these locations.

How did Abraham once again put in jeopardy God's promise to give him a son through Sarah? (Gen. 20:1, 2; see 12:10–15)

Notice how immediately and frontally God acted to preserve Sarah in spite of Abraham's deception. How did God rebuke Abimelech for taking Sarah into his harem? (Gen. 20:3)

In contrast, how did Abimelech rebuke Abraham for deceiving him and putting him in jeopardy? (Gen. 20:8, 9)

 BEHIND THE SCENES

Abimelech was a title rather than a proper name, just as Pharaoh is a title rather than a name. All the kings of the Philistine city Gerar apparently used Abimelech as a public title. "Abimelech" meant "My father, the king," and its use showed respect and reverence on the part of his subjects. In Genesis 26, Isaac and Rebekah will use the same ploy about their identities with King Abimelech of Gerar. But readers cannot tell whether Isaac dealt with the same Abimelech as Abraham or another king of Gerar with the same title. If they are different kings, they are both presented as upright rulers.

Compare the protestations of innocence by Abimelech and Abraham.

Abimelech (Gen. 20:4, 5)

Abraham (Gen. 20:11–13)

From Genesis 20:6–18, describe the confrontation between Abraham and Abimelech.

God's response to Abimelech's innocence

Abimelech's response to God's instruction

Abraham's response to Abimelech's actions

What does this incident teach about God's determination and ability to provide a son for Abraham and Sarah?

 FAITH ALIVE

Relate an incident in which the Lord protected you from your own folly so that you could carry out His plans for your life.

Abraham had to learn over and over that the Lord did not want him to use deception as a means of self-protection. What is a spiritual or moral lesson that you have found hard to get into your behavior pattern even though the Lord has taught it to you over and over?

1. Ronald F. Youngblood, *The Book of Genesis: An Introductory Commentary* (second edition; Grand Rapids, MI: Baker Book House, 1991), 160.

2. *Spirit-Filled Life Bible* (Nashville, TN: Thomas Nelson Publishers, 1991), 26, "Word Wealth: 15:6 accounted."

3. Ibid., 28, note on 12:1, 2.

4. Ibid., 29, "Kingdom Dynamics: The Words We Speak."

5. Ibid., 31, 32, "Kingdom Dynamics: Prayer Principles from God's Conversation with Abraham."

Lesson 8/The Son of Promise
(21:1—24:67)

In Stephen A. Lawhead's three-volume retelling of the legends of King Arthur, Arthur was a child of promise.[1] Long before prophesied by Taliesen, descendant of the survivors of Atlantis, the baby Arthur entered a hostile world.

According to the legend, those who expected Britain's salvation to come through Arthur were few, but many were his enemies among petty lords who would be high king. Worse still was the enmity of Morgan, the sorceress, whose wickedness also extended back to Atlantis.

As the story goes, on the night of Arthur's birth, the baby was smuggled from Uther Pendragon's castle by Merlin to be reared anonymously in the remote strongholds of loyal friends. Only when he had grown to young manhood would Arthur arrive at the council to claim the throne as his own by drawing the Sword of Britain from the stone where Merlin had thrust it years before.

At this point the Arthurian conflict between good and evil begins in earnest because it is out in the open. Always the reign of Arthur seems a breath away from destruction. There seem never enough human resources to battle the foes. In the end, only the sovereign power of the Living God was adequate to explain the preservation of the once and future king.

THE BIRTH AND HOME OF ISAAC

The son of promise was born into a family surrounded by the spiritually hostile culture of the Canaanites. The family itself contained a rival in the person of Abraham's son Ishmael, born to Sarah's Egyptian slave Hagar (see Gen. 16).

From Genesis 21:1–4, list the features concerning the birth of Isaac that had been predicted and record the references from the earlier chapters of Genesis in which the predictions occur.

PREDICTED FEATURE	REFERENCE
_____	_____
_____	_____
_____	_____
_____	_____
_____	_____
_____	_____

How did Sarah explain the choice of the name "Isaac" for her son? (Gen. 21:5–7)

What other incidents of laughter should the name "Isaac" have brought to his parents' minds? (Gen. 17:17; 18:12–15)

About how old was Ishmael when Isaac was born? (Reason from Gen. 17:25 and subsequent events)

How did Sarah determine that Ishmael could not share her home with Isaac? (Gen. 21:8–10)

How did Abraham decide how to respond to Sarah's displeasure with Ishmael? (Gen. 21:11–13)

How did Abraham provide for his son Ishmael when he sent him away? (Gen. 21:14)

How did the Lord provide for Abraham's son Ishmael when he sent him away? (Gen. 21:17–20)

 BIBLE EXTRA

The Submission That Bears Fruit (Sarah). Sarah, the beautiful (12:14) wife of Abraham, was barren (16:1), a condition considered a curse in the ancient world. She is a positive lesson 1) in faith that rises above personal limitations (Heb. 11:11) and 2) in a submitted spirit that responds biblically to her husband, without becoming depersonalized (1 Pet. 3:5, 6).

Sarah is also an illustration of the dangers of taking God's promises into our own hands. Her suggestion that Abraham take her handmaid as wife, in view of Sarah's barrenness, resulted in the birth of Ishmael—a child who occasioned jealousy and conflict between the two women, eventually between their two sons, and to this day, among their offspring.[2]

In what vicinity had Abraham continued to live during Sarah's pregnancy and Isaac's birth? (Gen. 21:22; see 20:1, 2)

Why did Abimelech want a treaty with Abraham? (Gen. 21:22)

What vow did Abimelech want from Abraham? (Gen. 21:23)

What was strange about a king and his captain making this request of a shepherd?

In return for his nonaggression pledge, what did Abraham ask of Abimelech? (Gen. 21:25–27)

What was the sign between Abraham and Abimelech that Beersheba belonged to Abraham? (Gen. 21:28–31)

WORD WEALTH

Beersheba is a compound name made up of *beer,* which means "well," and *sheba,* which means "seven." Beersheba is "the well of seven" (Gen. 21:28–30). In addition, *sheba* is very similar to the word for "oath," so Abraham and Abimelech could also assign Beersheba the meaning "well of the oath" (v. 31).

Why do you think Beersheba seemed like a good place for Abraham to settle down? (Gen. 21:32, 33)

FAITH ALIVE

How did the Lord provide a peaceful environment for the son of promise after his long-delayed birth?

How has the Lord provided peace in your life situation since your new birth in Christ? (Even if you have faced opposition in your Christian life, how has He provided peace?)

THE CONSECRATION OF ISAAC

The Lord had not given Abraham a peaceful life at Beersheba in order to make his life easy. It may have been to focus Abraham's mind and heart on God alone, because there came a day in which Abraham had to demonstrate what his faith was made of.

What was the purpose of God's demand of Abraham in Genesis 22? (v. 1)

 WORD WEALTH

The word "test" is a translation of the Hebrew verb *nasa.* "In most contexts *nasa* has the idea of testing or proving the quality of someone or something, often through adversity or hardship. The rendering *tempt,* used frequently by the AV and ASV, generally means 'prove, test, put to the test,' rather than the current English idea of 'entice to do wrong.' The verb *nasa* occurs 36 times in the OT. . . .

"*Nasa* is used when God tested Abraham (Gen. 22:1) and Hezekiah (2 Chr. 32:31). Such testing by God, however, was not without intent. It was to refine the character of man that he might walk more closely in God's ways."[3]

What does each descriptive phrase about Isaac in Genesis 22:2a add to the emotional impact of God's command to Abraham?

WORD WEALTH

"Only son" translates *yachid.* "*Yachid* describes Abraham's unique miracle child, Isaac. Zechariah describes what the Messiah will one day become to Israel's repentant, weeping citizens: a precious only son (Zech. 12:10). Here the place where God told Abraham to sacrifice his son Isaac is the same place where God sacrificed *His* own Son: the hills of Moriah in Jerusalem. Equally noteworthy is that the phrase 'His only begotten Son' in John 3:16 in the Hebrew New Testament is: 'His Son, His *Yachid.*'"[4]

Why do you think the Lord tested Abraham by commanding him to sacrifice Isaac as a burnt offering when He would clearly forbid child sacrifice as repugnant to Him? (Deut. 18:10)

From Genesis 22:6–10 describe Isaac's part in the sacrificial proceedings.

His conscious role

His unconscious role

His attitude when he knew what was going to happen

According to Genesis 22:3–10, what sorts of things did Abraham have to do before God stopped the test?

What did His test of Abraham reveal to God? (Gen. 22:11, 12)

What do you think God's provision of the ram in the thicket taught Abraham about Him?

What do you think this incident must have meant through the years to Abraham's son Isaac?

The Angel of the Lord probably was the second Person of the Trinity. What do you think this incident would have meant to God's Son?

What was Abraham's immediate reaction to the sacrifice? (Gen. 22:14)

What was the Lord's immediate reaction to the sacrifice? (Gen. 22:15–18)

 AT A GLANCE

The Abrahamic Covenant[5]	
Genesis 12:1–3	God initiated His covenant with Abram when he was living in Ur of the Chaldeans, promising a land, descendants, and blessing.
Genesis 12:4, 5	Abram went with his family to Haran, lived there for a time, and left at the age of 75.
Genesis 13:14–17	After Lot separated from Abram, God again promised the land to him and his descendants.
Genesis 15:1–21	This covenant was ratified when God passed between the sacrificial animals Abram laid before God.
Genesis 17:1–27	When Abram was 99 God renewed His covenant, changing Abram's name to Abraham ("Father of a Multitude"). Sign of the covenant: circumcision.
Genesis 22:15–18	Confirmation of the covenant because of Abraham's obedience.

The Abrahamic covenant was foundational to other covenants:
• The promise of land in the Palestinian Covenant (Deut. 30:1–10)
• The promise of kingly descendants in the Davidic Covenant (2 Sam. 7:12–16)
• The promise of blessing in the "Old" and "New" Covenants (Ex. 19:3–6; Jer. 31:31–40)

BIBLE EXTRA

Faith. Abraham's ability to lead was tested in three areas of faith: 1) *Faith to risk* (12:1–5): A wealthy man, Abraham risked all to follow God. The godly leader is willing to risk everything on God's faithfulness and venture into the unknown. 2) *Faith to trust* (17:1–27): Abraham and Sarah were long past the age of child-bearing. The godly leader does not rely on facts alone, but goes beyond facts to faith. 3) *Faith to surrender* (22:1–19): Abraham knew the sacrifice of his son would destroy any hope of fulfilling God's promise that he would father many nations. The godly leader is willing to sacrifice all things precious in order to please God.[6]

FAITH ALIVE

What has the Lord ever asked you to give up for His sake to reveal your character?

From your experience, give an example of surrendering something to God only to receive it back better than ever.

THE DEATH OF ISAAC'S MOTHER

Isaac, the son of promise, was part of a larger family in which he would find his place. The first tragedy in that family was the death of Sarah.

Who were Isaac's cousins born to his Uncle Nahor and Aunt Milcah? (Gen. 22:20–22)

Who was Isaac's second cousin who would play a large role in his life? (Gen. 22:23)

At the time of Sarah's death, how old were these characters?

Sarah (Gen. 23:1)

Abraham (see Gen. 17:17 for the difference between his age and Sarah's)

Isaac (see Gen. 17:17 for the difference between his age and Sarah's)

Where did Sarah die? (Gen. 23:2; see 13:18; 14:13)

How did Abraham characterize his status in the land of Canaan after living there for sixty-two years? (Gen. 23:4; see 12:4, 5)

Describe the colorful bedouin-style bargaining and posturing between Abraham and Ephron the Hittite. (Gen. 23:4–16)

Why do you think Abraham did not take Sarah back to Haran to be buried among their family with whom he had recently renewed contact?

In spite of Abraham's great wealth in livestock, the field and cave at Hebron were all the land he ever owned in Canaan. How does his purchase of this acreage show his confidence in the promise of God for Isaac and future generations? (see Gen. 13:14–18)

A BRIDE FOR ISAAC

After Sarah's death, Abraham turned his attention to locating a wife for Isaac. It was time for Isaac to start his family to further the growth of the people of promise. Abraham was ready to relinquish front stage in the drama of redemption to Isaac and his descendants.

From Genesis 24:2–9, describe Abraham's commission to his servant to find a wife for Isaac.

The seriousness of the mission (vv. 2, 3, 9)

The prohibitions of the mission (vv. 3, 6)

The goal of the mission (vv. 4, 7)

The reservations of the messenger (vv. 5, 8)

From Genesis 24:10–27, describe how the Lord directed Abraham's servant to Rebekah.

The setting of the encounter

The servant's prayer and its answer in Rebekah's actions

The servant's grateful worship

From Genesis 24:28–61, describe the decision of Rebekah to become the wife of Isaac.

The reception given Abraham's servant

The way the servant fulfilled the task given him by Abraham

The response of Rebekah's family

The urgency of the servant to depart

The decision of Rebekah about leaving

The family's blessing on Rebekah

 BIBLE EXTRA

The Blessing of an Unselfish Woman (Rebekah). A lesson in the way God provides surprising rewards for servant-spirited souls is seen in what happened to Rebekah. Little did she know those camels were carrying untold gifts for her and her family. Her will to wait for her family's blessing before accepting the invitation to leave for a marriage to Isaac, who was a wealthy prince of the ancient world, is a model for today. How many marriages today would be different 1) if the Holy Spirit were the guide, 2) if prayer and worship were the order of the day, and 3) if the couple had the blessing of the family?[7]

From Genesis 24:62–67, describe the marriage of Isaac and Rebekah.

The setting of their meeting (Gen. 16:6–14)

Isaac's frame of mind at their meeting

Rebekah's preparation for their meeting

The preparation of Isaac for their meeting (v. 63)

The relation of Isaac's marriage to the death of his mother

 FAITH ALIVE

Who has the Lord prepared to be a special blessing in your life as surely as He prepared Rebekah for Isaac, and how has that person blessed your life?

What can you learn from the habit of grateful worship by Abraham's servant that could help your spiritual life?

1. Stephen A. Lawhead, *The Pendragon Cycle* in 3 vol. (Winchester, IL: Crossway Books, 1987, 1988, and 1989).

2. *Spirit-Filled Life Bible* (Nashville, TN: Thomas Nelson Publishers, 1991), 28, "Kingdom Dynamics: The Submission That Bears Fruit (Sarah)."

3. Taken from *Theological Wordbook of the Old Testament,* Vol. 2, 581, edited by R. Laird Harris et al. Copyright © 1980, Moody Bible Institute of Chicago. Moody Press. Used by permission.

4. *Spirit-Filled Life Bible,* 36, "Word Wealth: 22:2 only son."

5. Ibid., 37, "Chart: The Abrahamic Covenant."

6. Ibid., 24, "Kingdom Dynamics: Faith."

7. Ibid., 39, "Kingdom Dynamics: The Blessing of an Unselfish Woman (Rebekah)."

Lesson 9/Selfishness Sown Among the People of Promise
(25:1—31:55)

Critics often call it his best play. Older actors lust for the emotional range to portray the lead character. But audiences find the tragedy almost overwhelming, so *King Lear* is not staged as often as lesser plays by Shakespeare.

In his old age, Lear dotes on his three daughters and expects them to dote on him as well. Two of the women gush all over the old man's foolish pride in order to advance their ambitions to gain control of large portions of their father's realm for their malleable husbands. The third, and favorite, daughter will not join the hypocrisy of her sisters in flattering her father. She loves him too much.

Aged Lear mistakes Cordelia's reluctance to fawn on his vanity as filial disloyalty, rashly disinherits her, and divides her third of his kingdom between her selfish and eager sisters. All of this happens rapidly in the opening scene of Act I.

The balance of *King Lear* portrays the disintegration of the old king's sanity as the horror of reality dawns on him. Goneril and Regan do not love or respect him. They contemptuously push the pathetic old man aside and strip him of all regal dignity. He has lost Cordelia's loyal love, his only hold on self-respect and stability, because he forced her into exile in France.

The seeds of Lear's bitter harvest were selfish ones. Lear's ambitious daughters understand his self-centeredness but not their own. Lear learns to his shame that Goneril and Regan want his power. When they have it, he is an annoyance to them, only fit to be discarded.

Almost a parallel in human experience, look at the contrasts of faith with selfishness. Against the shining backdrop of the faith of Abraham, Isaac and Jacob, though called to the covenant of the Lord, play out a sometimes distressingly selfish drama of family intrigue. How did Isaac survive the manipulation of Esau by Jacob? How did Jacob fare against his Uncle Laban who could match him greedy trick for greedy trick? What was the Lord going to do with these people who were supposed to bless the whole world?

SELF-PROTECTION IN ABRAHAM'S FAMILY

Self-protection can be the prudent action of a wise man, or it can be the scheming wile of a fox. Note all the variations between the two extremes of self-protection in Genesis 25 and 26.

How did Abraham protect Isaac from any legal claim on his inheritance by the sons of his second wife and his concubines? (Gen. 25:1–6)

Based on your calculation in the last lesson of people's ages at the time of Sarah's death, how many years passed between her death and Abraham's? (Gen. 25:7)

How old was Isaac when Abraham died?

Why do you think only Ishmael and Isaac of Abraham's sons were to bury him? (Gen. 25:9)

Why do you think Isaac chose to live at Beer Lahai Roi instead of Hebron or Beersheba where his parents had lived during his earlier years? (Gen. 25:11; see 16:7–14; 24:62–67)

How did the Lord's predictions about Ishmael come true? (Gen. 16:12; 21:17–21; 25:12–18)

From Genesis 25:19–28, describe the beginning of the family of Isaac and Rebekah.

Similarity of Rebekah's experience to Sarah's

Similarities between the relationships of Esau to Jacob and Ishmael to Isaac

Dissimilarities between the relationships of Esau to Jacob and Ishmael to Isaac

Stated and implied reasons Isaac might have favored Esau over Jacob

Stated and implied reasons Rebekah might have favored Jacob over Esau

Dangers posed for the family by Isaac and Rebekah's favoritism

 BEHIND THE SCENES

The names of Isaac and Rebekah's twin boys had meaning, as did most Hebrew names. The name "Esau" was suggested by the baby's hairy appearance. While the name "Esau" does not mean "hairy," it sounds like the word that does and so suggests that meaning.

> "*Jacob,* an existing name found elsewhere, means 'May he be at the heels'—i.e., 'May God be your rear guard.' But it also lends itself to a hostile sense, of dogging another's steps, or overreaching, as Esau bitterly observed in 27:36. Through his own actions Jacob devalued the name into a synonym for treachery."[1]

From Genesis 25:29–34, what do you learn about the values, character, and cunning of Isaac and Rebekah's twins?

Esau

Jacob

From Genesis 26:1–16, what do you learn about Isaac's relationship to the Lord and to people around him?

What the Lord said to Isaac

What Isaac said to people around

How the Lord prospered Isaac

How people resented Isaac

How Isaac's deception may have contributed to the popular resentment of him?

From Genesis 26:17–25, describe Isaac's ongoing relationships with people and the Lord.

With people

With the Lord

How did the blessing of the Lord earn Isaac the reluctant respect of people around him? (Gen. 26:26–33)

HOSTILITY BETWEEN JACOB AND ESAU

Even though the Lord communicated clearly with Isaac, there didn't seem to be much clear and honest communication among the members of his family. Each family member seems to have followed a course of action to get what he or she wanted, even at the expense of other family members.

From Genesis 26:34—27:29, describe how Jacob received the blessing Isaac meant for Esau.

How Esau deeply hurt his parents

Why Isaac still planned to bless Esau

How Rebekah planned to get the blessing for her favorite

The moral inadequacy of Jacob's objection to her plan

The lies Jacob had to tell to pull it off

The blessing Jacob stole

From Genesis 27:30–41, describe how Isaac and Esau reacted to the theft of the blessing by Jacob.

Isaac's emotional response

Esau's emotional response

Isaac's description of the theft

Esau's description of the theft

Esau's secondary blessing

Esau's plan for revenge

From Genesis 27:42—28:9, describe the next round of deception in Isaac's household.

Rebekah's fear

Rebekah's scheme

How she tricked Isaac into carrying it out

Esau's rash reaction

In spite of Jacob's deceit in taking the birthright and the blessing from Esau, the Lord chose to establish His covenant with him. Refer to the map in Lesson 6 on page 66 for the locations along Jacob's journey as you describe, from Genesis 28:10–22, Jacob's life-changing encounter with the Lord at Bethel.

Jacob's plan for the night

Jacob's dream

The Lord's covenant

Jacob's reaction to his dream

Jacob's vow (Note that Jacob's tithing here predates the Law and thereby stands as a timeless principle of godly practice.)

HOSTILITY BETWEEN JACOB'S WIVES

In Haran, Jacob was tricked by his uncle into marrying both cousins when he loved only one of them. Jacob then experienced the consequences of being on the receiving end of deception in the form of strained relations between his wives.

Compare Genesis 29:1–14 with 24:10–31. Compare and contrast Jacob's arrival in Haran with that of Abraham's servant.

Similarities of the events

Differences between the events

From Genesis 29:15–30, describe the deception of Jacob by Laban in terms of these topics:

The motivations of Laban's deceit

How Laban's deceit was like Jacob's theft of Esau's blessing

The inadequacy of Laban's explanation for his deceit

The goals of Laban's deceit

Why did the Lord initially grant children to Leah and withhold them from Rachel? (Gen. 29:31)

How did childless Rachel compete with Leah for Jacob's affection? (Gen. 30:1–4)

What was Leah's response to Rachel's ploy? (Gen. 30:9)

What did the incident with Reuben's mandrakes, a supposed fertility-enhancing plant, reveal about Leah and Rachel's relationship with one another and with Jacob? (Gen. 29:31—30:16)

Fill in the chart below about the first twelve of Jacob's children. (Gen. 29:31—30:24)

NAME	MOTHER	MEANING OF NAME

FAITH ALIVE

What happens inside a family when its members feel like they have to perform well to be accepted by one another?

What can you do as a Christlike peacemaker to reduce or prevent competition for affection within your immediate or extended family?

HOSTILITY BETWEEN JACOB AND LABAN

Jacob and Laban were too much alike to get along well. Eventually their jockeying for advantage over one another produced enough tension to lead to the parting of their ways.

What did Jacob and Uncle Laban say to one another's faces about their separation? (Gen. 30:25–28)

Jacob

Laban

What were Jacob and Uncle Laban actually thinking about one another? (Gen. 31:38–43)

Jacob

Laban

From Genesis 30:29—31:2, describe Jacob's proposal for his wages.

What he asked for

How he manipulated his share

Results in terms of wealth

Results in terms of hostility

From Genesis 31:3–21, describe Jacob's departure from Haran and Uncle Laban.

Jacob's description of Laban

Jacob's description of the Lord's directions

Leah and Rachel's response

The departure

What can you conclude about Rachel's spiritual understanding at this time? (Gen. 30:14, 15, 22–24; 31:19)

From Genesis 31:22–42, describe Uncle Laban's pursuit of Jacob.

His intent

God's intervention

His complaint

The danger from the idols

Jacob's indignant rebuke

From Genesis 31:43–55, describe the covenant of peace between the reluctant participants Jacob and Uncle Laban.

The sign of the covenant

The purpose of the covenant

Laban's warning to Jacob

Appeal to God and ceremony

Separation scene

FAITH ALIVE

Why is it hard for scheming people to have friends?

Why do people close to schemers tend to become schemers themselves (as did Rachel)?

Like everyone else, schemers reap what they sow. What built-in judgments do you think scheming people face?

In their families

In their friendships

In their working relationships

1. Taken from *Genesis* (TOTC) by Derek Kidner. © 1967 by Tyndale Press. Used by permission of InterVarsity Press, P.O. Box 1400, Downers Grove, IL 60515.

Lesson 10/Hatred Harvested Among the People of Promise
(32:1—36:43)

As tragic as the seeds of selfishness sown by his family were for old King Lear, they were nothing compared to the harvest of hatred he and his greedy daughters Goneril and Regan reaped. Edmund, illegitimate son of the Earl of Gloucester, recognizes the greed of Goneril and Regan and begins to woo them with pretended love. His goal is to become king of England.

Meanwhile, rejected but loyal Cordelia has married the king of France with the goal of restoring the glory of her father who has been reduced to an unwelcome guest in one or the other sister's castle. Cordelia invades England, so Goneril and Regan form an uneasy alliance to defeat the French army.

All the suspicion, jealousy, and hatred that have festered in King Lear's family erupt during the climactic battle. Cordelia's army is defeated, and Edmund orders the murder of Cordelia and Lear. Goneril and Regan discover they both desire Edmund and die a murder-suicide.

Lear is saved from execution to find all of his daughters dead. Even in the shadow lands of insanity, he grieves:

Howl, howl, howl, howl! Oh, you are men of stone.
Had I your tongues and eyes, I'd use them so
That heaven's vault should crack.[1]

These dramatic words prompt our questioning what similar emotions might erupt as we turn to the Scriptures and see Jacob and Esau about to meet again after twenty years.

What would Jacob find when he faced his brother Esau who had vowed to kill him in revenge for stealing his blessing? What would Jacob's children be like, reared as they were against the backdrop of the competition between their mothers and the intrigue between their father and Laban? Would Jacob begin to share the despair of King Lear because of the inexorable hateful reaping that follows selfish sowing? Would the Lord in His mercy raise up a more successful deliverer for Jacob than Cordelia proved to be for Lear?

JACOB'S UNEASY PEACE WITH HIS BROTHER

Jacob was terrified at the prospect of facing Esau again. He plotted and schemed how to appease Esau's wrath. Fortunately, the Lord intervened to draw Jacob's attention to His presence and protection.

From Genesis 32:1–8, describe Jacob's communication with his estranged brother Esau.

Source of Jacob's courage to contact Esau

Jacob's message to Esau

Esau's response

Jacob's plan for meeting Esau

From Genesis 32:9–21, describe Jacob's approaches to God and to Esau at his time of crisis.

Form of addressing God

Form of addressing Esau

What Jacob wanted from God

What Jacob wanted from Esau

The basis of Jacob's appeal to God

The basis of Jacob's appeal to Esau

From Genesis 32:22–32, describe Jacob's wrestling match with the "Man" (see Hos. 12:4).

The situation

How the "Man" prevailed against Jacob

How Jacob prevailed against the "Man"

How Jacob understood the event

How would Jacob's encounter with the "Man" prepare him for his encounter with Esau?

From Genesis 33:1–11, describe Jacob's actual reunion with Esau.

Jacob's anxious preparation

Esau's emotional greeting

The haggling over Jacob's gift

From Genesis 33:12–20, describe Jacob's disengagement from Esau

Esau's offers of companionship

Jacob's evasions of Esau's offers

Jacob's course of action

What reasons might Jacob have had for distrusting Esau's emotional welcome and invitation to accompany him to Seir?

From Genesis 33:18–20, describe the permanent home Jacob established in the Promised Land according to these topics.

Location

Permanence

Worship (see 12:6, 7)

 FAITH ALIVE

What were Jacob's chances for reconciliation with Esau after these events?

If Jacob had wanted a real reconciliation with Esau, what would he have needed to do?

What are the risks any Christian faces in trying to achieve reconciliation with an estranged family member who does not know the Lord as both Savior and Lord?

JACOB'S UNCERTAIN CONTROL OF HIS SONS

It must have seemed wonderful to Jacob when he had survived the hurdle of encountering Esau and was settled in the land promised to him by the God of his fathers Abraham and Isaac (Gen. 28:13, 14). Soon he found that his greatest danger was not from external enemies but from the harvest of hatred springing up in his family from the seeds of selfishness.

From Genesis 34:1–12, describe the rape of Jacob's daughter, Dinah, by Shechem.

How it happened

Shechem's response

Jacob's response

Jacob's sons' response

Hamor's proposition

Shechem's fateful promise

Contrast the character of the sons of Jacob (Gen. 34:13) with that of the pagan rapist, Shechem (v. 19).

What trick did the sons of Jacob use to incapacitate the men of Shechem? (Gen. 34:13–17)

How was this use of circumcision inconsistent with its God-ordained purpose? (see Gen. 17:10–14)

How did Hamor and Shechem convince the men of the city to consent to circumcision? (Gen. 34:20–24)

Consult the chart of Jacob's children on page 109 of Lesson 9. Why were Simeon and Levi motivated to revenge Dinah?

How did Simeon and Levi revenge the rape of Dinah? (Gen. 34:25, 26)

How did the rest of Jacob's sons join in the violence? (Gen. 34:27–29)

What was Jacob's response to the vengeance of Simeon and Levi? (Gen. 34:30)

What things were wrong with Jacob's responses to the rape of Dinah (Gen. 34:5) and the massacre by Simeon and Levi? (v. 30) How is the rebuke offered Jacob by his blood-thirsty sons justified? (v. 31)

 FAITH ALIVE

What are the spiritual and personal dangers posed to children by parents who avoid dealing with major conflicts with other people?

How do family members lose respect for one another when they see reactions to problems that are contrary to the faith in God they all profess?

How does the Spirit of God warn you that you are setting a bad spiritual example for those closest to you?

JACOB'S CONSOLATION IN HIS GRIEF

Jacob's griefs at the hands of his sons were just beginning, but Jacob was spared the insanity of a King Lear by reason of the mercy of God. As Jacob entered a time marked by the death of loved ones, the Lord sustained him.

After the disaster at Shechem, how did God redirect the life of Jacob? (Gen. 35:1; see 28:10–22)

From Genesis 35:2–15, describe Jacob's return to Bethel.

Purification of the household

Response of surrounding people

Worship

Renaming of Jacob

Promises to Jacob

AT A GLANCE

Complete the following chart to get an overview of the altar building that the patriarchs engaged in as they wandered as pilgrims in the Promised Land.

GENESIS	PATRIARCH	PLACE	NAME OF GOD
12:6, 7			
12:8			
13:18			
22:2, 9			
26:23–25			
33:18–20			
35:1, 7			

The God whom the patriarchs worshiped by means of these altars in the Book of Genesis wants to be known. "Commanding, conversing and, above all, entering into covenant, He is always in some degree self-giving, never the aloof object of human groping."[2]

Look up the following passages and note other names by which the Lord revealed Himself in Genesis.

14:18–22 _____

16:13 _____

17:1 _____

21:33 _____

31:42, 53 _____

49:24 _____

From Genesis 35:16–20, describe the death of Rachel.

Location

Cause

Rachel and Jacob's emotional states reflected in the baby's names

Memorial

While Jacob was mourning the death of his favored wife and finding solace in her baby, what was his oldest son by the unfavored wife up to? (Gen. 35:22, 25)

Jacob did not deal with Reuben's incest, even as he had vacillated when Shechem raped Dinah, but he did not forget. Later Jacob would hold Reuben accountable.

From Genesis 35:27–29, describe the reunion of Isaac's family and his death.

The place

Isaac's age

Esau and Jacob's age (see 25:26)

Isaac's burial

Chapter 35 records the deaths of Deborah, Rachel, and Isaac. What do you think each of these three deaths meant to Jacob at this stage of his life?

35:8

35:16–20

35:29

What had to worry Jacob after Isaac's death? (Gen. 27:41)

From Genesis 36:1–43, what can you infer about Esau's family?

In terms of size

In terms of success

In terms of organization

In terms of territory

When Esau's genealogy is compared to Jacob's (Gen. 35:23–26), why might you suppose that Esau did not revenge himself on Jacob, even if Esau continued to dislike him?

 FAITH ALIVE

How has the Lord made His sustaining presence known to you during times of distress?

What places, times, or events in your life function like Bethel did for Jacob — things to go back to physically or spiritually for renewal and strengthening?

---

1. William Shakespeare, *King Lear*, V, iii, 257–259.

2. Taken from *Genesis* (TOTC) by Derek Kidner. © 1967 by Tyndale Press. Used by permission of InterVarsity Press, P.O. Box 1400, Downers Grove, IL 60515.

Lesson 11/A Savior for the People of Promise
(37:1—41:57)

As alluded to in Lesson 8, King Arthur of English legends was a child of promise. Arthur also was a savior for Britain. He represented the civilization of the original Britons, cultivated by Roman conquerors and colonists, that was threatened by the barbaric Angles, Saxons, and other invading tribes.

Legend persists that Arthur united the fractious British warlords into a force that repeatedly repelled the fierce Saxons and their allies. Arthur's England became Tennyson's idyllic place of chivalry and noble quests. At Arthur's round table justice and honor flowered among a band of knights committed to righteous causes. Among Arthur's royal residences Camelot captures the imagination as the expression in architecture and government of the beauty and harmony implicit in all he did.

The longer Arthur combated evil, the more directly evil opposed him. Initially evil appeared in barbaric hordes; eventually it came openly in the person of the relentlessly cunning Mordred. Finally Mordred mortally wounded Arthur in a battle that cost him his life as well. The final note of hope in the Arthurian tales is that Arthur waits in mythic Avalon until the hour of England's greatest need when he will return to save her again, England's once and future king.

Again, a fictional tale provides an interesting analogy to the people of promise. For now we see Jacob's family needed a savior from the hatred that was springing up everywhere from the selfish seeds sown in most personal interactions. So God now raises up Joseph, one of Rachel's sons, to be an agent of change among his brothers.

But there will be no Arthurian "magic" for Joseph in rescuing his brothers from themselves. Instead there will be a tremendous price of suffering for Joseph to pay over a period of years when there seems no reason to expect anything good to ever come from it.

Joseph Betrayed by His Brothers

As a teenager Joseph wasn't ready to be a family savior. He may well have been a spoiled child who irritated his volatile older brothers so that they hated him. Then as now it took suffering to produce a saint who could have dramatic impact on other people.

From Genesis 37:1–11, describe Joseph's relationship with his brothers.

Family home (see v. 14)

Joseph's age

Who he tattled on (see 30:5–13)

Jacob's favoritism

Joseph's first dream

Joseph's second dream

How do you think Joseph should have handled the information about his dreams? (Gen. 37:5–11)

BEHIND THE SCENES

Being the firstborn of Jacob's favorite wife, Rachel, Joseph not surprisingly became his favorite son. We do not know the correct description of this tunic of many colors. The translation here follows the Septuagint's "many colors," but it may be "a long robe with sleeves." An inscription from another Semitic language, Akkadian, suggests "an ornamented tunic," as might be worn by royalty.[1]

AT A GLANCE

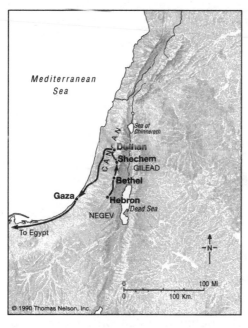

This map shows the places involved in Joseph's search for his brothers and their flocks and his sale into slavery in Egypt.[2]

From Genesis 37:12–20, describe Joseph's fateful encounter with his brothers.

Why Jacob may have been concerned about his older sons (see 34:25–30)

Why Joseph's errand might have irritated his brothers (see v. 2)

How Joseph found his brothers

How his brothers reacted to seeing Joseph coming

From Genesis 37:21–30, contrast the roles of Reuben and Judah in Joseph's fate.

Their birth order and its significance

Their motives

Traces of compassion

Their guilt for Joseph's sale

 BEHIND THE SCENES

    The merchants who purchased Joseph for sale as a slave are called both Midianites and Ishmaelites (Gen. 37:28). Technically Midianites were descendants of Abraham's son by his second wife Keturah (25:1), and Ishmaelites were descendants of Abraham's son by Hagar, Sarah's Egyptian maid (25:12–18).
    "It appears . . . that 'Ishmaelite' was an inclusive term for Israel's nomadic cousins (Ishmael was the senior offshoot from Abraham), somewhat as 'Arab' embraces numerous

tribes in our way of speaking, and can alternate with one of their names without awkwardness."[3] See Judges 8:24 for another example of the inclusion of Midianite within the larger "family" of Ishmaelites.

From Genesis 37:31–36, describe the conclusion of the disposal of Joseph.

The brothers' coverup

Jacob's reaction

Joseph's destination

JUDAH: PORTRAIT OF A TRAITOR

What sort of person was Judah that he could callously sell his younger brother? Was there any hint in his character that he might be open to the action of God's Spirit to transform him into a godly man?

Describe how Judah established his family. (Gen. 38:1–5)

From Genesis 38:6–11, what do you know about these members of Judah's family?

Er

Onan

Selah

Tamar

From Genesis 38:12–26, describe how Tamar got Judah's attention.

Tamar's opportunity

Tamar's tactic

How Judah put his reputation in Tamar's hands

Tamar's peril

Judah's exposure

Judah's admission

 BEHIND THE SCENES

The **signet** was a personal identification seal hanging from a **cord** about its owner's neck. The **staff** probably had a distinctive carving at the top. Tamar had a sense for the dramatic; she knew that anyone in the household could quickly identify their owner.[4]

What base and noble qualities struggled within Judah like the twins within Tamar?

Base qualities

Noble qualities

How does the birth of Tamar's twins (Gen. 38:27–30) picture the turmoil of Judah's household?

In the light of Genesis 38, why is it not surprising that Judah took the lead in betraying Joseph?

 FAITH ALIVE

Who in your Christian circles was once a rascal who seemed an unlikely candidate for sainthood? How has the Lord's Spirit transformed that person?

Whom do you know now who seems unlikely ever to surrender to God's grace? How might you pray for that "hopeless case"?

PURIFIED BY SUFFERING

Meanwhile in Egypt, Joseph went through a series of difficulties that would have broken a person who had no faith in God. These experiences purged away the youthful boasting of a father's favorite son.

From Genesis 39:1–6, describe Joseph's situation as a slave in Egypt.

Joseph's master

Potiphar's assessment of Joseph

Joseph's responsibilities

The outcome of Joseph's service

From Genesis 39:7–20, describe Joseph's fall from favor with Potiphar.

Potiphar's wife's proposition

Joseph's response

Potiphar's wife's physical advance

Joseph's response

Potiphar's wife's revenge on Joseph

Potiphar's action

How were the motive and action of Potiphar's wife similar to those of Joseph's brothers?

How did the Lord bless Joseph in prison? (Gen. 39:21–23)

From Genesis 40, describe Joseph's frustrated opportunity to escape his unjust imprisonment.

Why there were new prisoners

Why Joseph was involved with them

How Joseph became their spiritual advisor

The butler's dream

Joseph's interpretation of the butler's dream

The baker's dream

Joseph's interpretation of the baker's dream

According to Genesis 40:20–23, what were the results of Joseph's dream interpretations?

For the butler

For the baker

For Joseph

What do you think kept Joseph from becoming discouraged and angry and from giving up when everything always worked out unfairly for him?

FAITH ALIVE

How does God use suffering to expose sin and immaturity in our lives?

What risk does God take when He permits suffering to enter our lives as a means of purification?

Tell of an instance when suffering has been the agent of the Holy Spirit in strengthening your Christian life.

EXALTED TO EASE SUFFERING

When the Lord knew that Joseph was spiritually ready to handle the task He had for him without pride, the Lord brought Joseph to a position of power. From that position Joseph would humbly save multitudes of starving people from many nations.

From Genesis 41:1–8, describe Pharaoh's troubling dreams.

Their relative time of occurrence

Their content

Their problem

BEHIND THE SCENES

Dreams were assumed to be messages from God (see Job 7:14). The ancient Egyptians left many hieroglyphic writings with detailed instructions on how to **interpret** dreams; thus **the magicians** and **wise men** were experienced to understand what God was telling Pharaoh. The magicians were expected to be experts in handling the ritual books of magic.[5]

From Genesis 41:9–36, describe Joseph's involvement with Pharaoh's dreams.

The butler's account of Joseph's abilities

Joseph's account of his abilities

Joseph's interpretation of Pharaoh's dreams

Joseph's recommended response to the dreams

From Genesis 41:37–45, describe Pharaoh's promotion of Joseph to coordinate the famine relief project.

Reasons Pharaoh selected Joseph

Responsibilities given Joseph

Authority and honors given Joseph

 BEHIND THE SCENES

Restoration Foreshadowed. The outline of God's restoration work stands out vividly in the life of Joseph. Joseph was *forsaken, falsely accused,* and *forgotten.* But finally he was *favored* by God and restored to the rule God had ordained for him.

1. *Forsaken.* When Joseph revealed to his brothers that God had called him to rule over them, they reacted with vicious envy, selling him into slavery in Egypt.

2. *Falsely Accused.* God prospered Joseph—even in slavery, so that his master put him in charge of his estate. But then his master's wife falsely accused Joseph of assaulting her, and he was thrown into prison.

3. *Forgotten.* While in prison, Joseph interpreted the dreams of Pharaoh's butler and baker. The butler was elated at hearing he would be set free, and Joseph asked him to speak a good word for him to Pharaoh. But, once out of prison and doing well, the butler forgot Joseph.

4. *Favored.* God did not forget, however. Two years later Pharaoh had a dream. The butler remembered Joseph and told Pharaoh about him. Joseph interpreted the dream, warning Pharaoh of seven years of famine. Grateful for the warning, Pharaoh put Joseph in control of all the wealth of Egypt. Not only was Joseph restored by this act, but, when the drought struck, he was in a position to save his people.[6]

About how long had Joseph been in Egypt before the Lord exalted him? (Gen. 41:46 in comparison with 37:2)

What was Joseph's strategy for preparing for the seven years of famine? (Gen. 41:46–49)

What happened in Joseph's personal life during the seven years of plenty? (Gen. 41:50–52)

According to Genesis 41:53–57, what were the responses of various people when the famine hit?

The Egyptians

Pharaoh

Joseph

Surrounding nations

FAITH ALIVE

From your observation, how does God generally prepare His children for major responsibilities in the church or other Christian organizations?

Why is pride such a difficult spiritual enemy for leaders, especially young ones like Joseph?

If the Lord doesn't take a leader through suffering, how else might He teach that leader to be humble?

1. *Spirit-Filled Life Bible* (Nashville, TN: Thomas Nelson Publishers, 1991), 59, note on 37:3.
2. Ibid., map on 60.
3. Taken from *Genesis* (TOTC) by Derek Kidner. © 1967 by Tyndale Press. Used by permission of InterVarsity Press, P.O. Box 1400, Downers Grove, IL 60515.
4. *Spirit-Filled Life Bible*, 62, note on 38:25.
5. Ibid., 64, note on 41:8.
6. Ibid., 2013, "Kingdom Dynamics: The Holy Spirit and Restoration."

Lesson 12/Patriarchs for the People of Promise
(42:1—45:28)

Pastor Marks paused by the bulletin board in the church office and transferred the list of church members in the area hospitals from the posted chart to his memo book. "Ruth, when did Gerry Young go into City Hospital?" he asked the church receptionist.

"The hospital called this morning to say he was there," Ruth answered. "Wasn't this something scheduled?"

"No. I think I'd better call Sheila and see what's wrong."

But Mrs. Young wasn't home, so Pastor Marks headed for the hospital. City was only twenty minutes from the church, so Pastor Marks didn't have much time to wonder. In the car he prayed for Gerry, Sheila, and their two teen-aged sons.

Gerry Young was a lot more than a member of the church. He was a friend, and practically a colleague in the ministry. As a Christian psychiatrist, he was a valuable ally in really difficult counseling situations.

Sheila Young answered his knock on the hospital room door. "Pastor Marks, what are you doing here so soon? We just got into this room about an hour ago. The emergency room people were great, but I thought we'd never get out of there."

"The hospital called the church this morning," Pastor Marks said. They processed your paper work faster than your patient. Speaking of which, what's going on here, Gerry?" Pastor Marks had made his way past Mrs. Young to the bedside where his friend lay.

Gerry's face was gray with pain, and his breathing was shallow and rapid. He forced a smile, but as he got right beside the bed Pastor Marks could see a line of sweat beads on his friend's forehead.

"Kidney stone, Reverend"

"I'm sorry to hear that." And he was, although Pastor Marks was also relieved that Gerry faced more pain than danger.

"It's funny," Gerry went on. "I've practiced psychiatry nearly twenty-five years and I've never been a patient in one of these places. I've been in here hundreds of times but always standing where you are. I hate this pain, but I think it'll make me a better doctor."

Gerry closed his eyes and licked his dry lips so he could smile again. "It had better. I don't want to go through this for nothing."

JOSEPH'S BROTHERS EXPERIENCE HIS PAIN

When the seven-year famine struck the Middle East during the enslavement of Joseph in Egypt, his brothers were forced to come to him as the controller of the only adequate food supply in the region. The ordeal Joseph put his brothers through was not vindictive. It was God's means of awakening their consciences so that they would acknowledge their guilt and repent.

From Genesis 42:1–5, describe the decision of Joseph's family to buy food from Egypt.

Jacob's approach to his older sons

Jacob's approach to Benjamin

The traveling circumstances

From Genesis 42:6–13, describe Joseph's initial encounter with his brothers.

How the brothers approached Joseph

How Joseph approached the brothers

What Joseph remembered and why

What Joseph accused the brothers of

How the brothers described themselves

How was the accusation of Joseph against his brothers (vv. 9, 12) similar to a grudge they had held against him? (37:2)

How could the brothers demonstrate their innocence of Joseph's spy charges against them? (Gen. 42:14, 15)

What choice did the brothers have to think about for three days under Joseph's first plan? (Gen. 42:16, 17)

Why was a prison cell an appropriate place symbolically for this deliberation?

What was the second choice Joseph forced his brothers to make when he changed the terms of his plan? (Gen. 42:18–20)

Whom did the brothers choose to stay as hostage until Benjamin could come to Egypt and prove their innocence? (Gen. 42:20, 24)

What did this ordeal force the brothers to remember? (Gen. 42:21, 22)

Why do you think this situation caused them to recall what they had done to Joseph?

What was Joseph's reaction to the guilt and stress his brothers were experiencing? (Gen. 42:23, 24)

From Genesis 42:25–38, describe the homecoming of Joseph's brothers.

The perceived problem created by the presence of the money in the grain sacks

The accuracy of the report to Jacob by his notoriously dishonest sons

Jacob's reaction to the report of his sons

Reuben's proposal

What are your impressions of firstborn Reuben as the leader of his brothers? (see Gen. 37:21, 22, 29, 30; 42:22, 37)

FAITH ALIVE

When has the Spirit of God brought back to your memory a sin hidden in your past that He wanted you to deal with?

How did the Lord bring your forgotten guilt to your attention?

What did He want you to do to deal with that guilt?

THE BROTHERS EXPERIENCE THEIR FATHER'S PAIN

Not only had Joseph's brothers caused tremendous suffering in his life, but they had caused decades of grief for their father Jacob by letting him think that Joseph had been killed by wild animals. On their first trip to Egypt, the brothers were faced with the anguish they had put Joseph through. On the second trip, they have to confront the pain they have caused their father.

From Genesis 43:1–7, describe the problem in Jacob's household.

Jacob's command

Judah's reminder

Jacob's complaint

The brothers' defense

From Genesis 43:8–14, describe Jacob's decision to send Benjamin to Egypt with his brothers.

Judah's proposal

Jacob's shrewdness in business matters

Jacob's resignation in family matters

Read through Genesis 43 and 44 and underline all of the occurrences of the name *Judah*. What do you conclude about Judah from this frequency?

From Genesis 43:15–25, describe the return to Egypt of Joseph's brothers.

Joseph's reaction to seeing Benjamin

The brothers' interpretation of Joseph's action

Their defense to Joseph's steward

Joseph's steward's actions

From Genesis 43:26–34, describe Joseph's meal with his brothers.

The brothers' fear of Joseph

Joseph's emotional involvement in this event

How Joseph kept his brothers wary of him

How Joseph honored his brothers

From Genesis 44:1–17, describe Joseph's final ordeal for his brothers.

The trap Joseph set for his brothers

The orders Joseph gave his servants

The defense of the innocent brothers

The horror of the search

The attitude of the brothers to Joseph

Joseph's sentence on Benjamin

What do you think Joseph was trying to accomplish with his brothers by insisting that he practiced divination, or fortune-telling? (Gen. 44:5, 15)

What do you think Judah meant when he said to Joseph, "God has found out the iniquity of your servants"? (Gen. 44:16)

Explain the irony in Joseph's dismissal of Judah, "And as for you, go up in peace to your father." (Gen. 44:17)

    FAITH ALIVE

Why do you think it is difficult for children, even grown ones, to appreciate the pressures and pains their parents experience?

How is understanding parental pressures and pains a way in which children can honor their parents?

JUDAH ACCEPTS FULL RESPONSIBILITY

This is the climax of God's behind-the-scenes work in the lives of Jacob's crafty, violent sons. From this moment there can be no doubt that Judah is the leader of the sons of Jacob.

How did Judah accept responsibility for Benjamin's being in Egypt at all? (Gen. 44:18–26)

How did Judah show deep insight into his father's concern for Benjamin? (Gen. 44:27–31)

How did Judah establish that it was appropriate for him to take Benjamin's place? (Gen. 44:32)

From Genesis 44:33, 34, describe Judah's appeal to Joseph to let him take Benjamin's place in slavery.

His attitude toward Benjamin

His attitude toward Jacob

Contrast the offers to take Benjamin's place made by Reuben (Gen. 42:37) and by Judah (44:33).

Contrast Judah's attitudes shown in Genesis 37:26–35 and 44:18–34.

Toward his father's favorite son

Toward his father

Toward what is important to him

FAITH ALIVE

Tell of an instance in which you have seen Christian love motivate someone to take on himself or herself the burdens, misfortunes, or punishment of someone else in order to help that person.

Why do you think substitutionary love is so spiritually powerful in helping people respond to God?

HIS BROTHERS EXALTED BY JOSEPH

The moment arrived that Joseph had hoped for. He could reveal who he was, but there was no easy way to do so after all of the trials he had put his brothers through to be God's agent of change in their lives.

What did Joseph have to do before he could reveal himself to his brothers? (Gen. 45:1, 2)

In regard to his emotions

In regard to the Egyptians

What was the initial reaction of the brothers to Joseph's self-revelation? (Gen. 45:3)

Why do you think Joseph had his brothers approach before identifying himself again? (Gen. 45:4; see 43:32)

Why do you think Joseph wanted it out in the open from the start of his new relationship with his brothers that once they had sold him into slavery? (Gen. 45:4)

How did Joseph want his brothers to look at the sale-into-slavery episode? (Gen. 45:5–8)

Negatively

Positively

What message did Joseph send to Jacob by means of his brothers? (Gen. 45:9–11)

Concerning himself

Concerning Jacob's future

What charge did Joseph give his brothers concerning Jacob? (Gen. 45:13)

How did Joseph conclude his self-revelation to his brothers? (Gen. 45:14, 15)

BIBLE EXTRA

Love Embraces Those Who Have Wronged Us. The story of Joseph is an early account of the forgiving nature God expects us to display in our treatment of those who have wronged us. It is a founding example of Christ-like love. . . .

Joseph's forgiveness of his brothers' sin is so complete that he kisses all of them and weeps with joy at being united with them once again. Brotherly love is expressive, self-giving, and offered in a way that assists its being received.[1]

How did Pharaoh respond to the report that Joseph's family had come to see him? (Gen. 45:16–20)

How did Joseph honor his brothers and father when he sent his brothers home? (Gen. 45:21–24)

How did Joseph's brothers convince Jacob that Joseph was still alive? (Gen. 45:25–27)

How did Jacob respond to the news that Joseph was alive and governing Egypt? (Gen. 45:26–28)

 FAITH ALIVE

Forgiveness is not the spiritual grace you exercise toward people who annoy you or who accidentally offend you. Forbearance is the old-fashioned term for the grace that you need to direct at them (Col. 3:13). Forgiveness is bestowed on people who betray you and are disloyal to you.

Frankly, there are many Christians who refuse to forgive. They take perverse pleasure in nurturing grudges, unaware that they are poisoning their spiritual lives (I Iob. 11:15).

What sorts of offenses do you find hard to forgive the offender?

What sorts of offenders do you find hard to forgive?

What did you learn about forgiveness from Joseph's treatment of his brothers that can help you be more forgiving?

1. *Spirit-Filled Life Bible* (Nashville, TN: Thomas Nelson Publishers, 1991), 71, "Kingdom Dynamics: Love Embraces Those Who Have Wronged Us."

Lesson 13/Peace Among the People of Promise
(46:1—50:26)

Remember *Gone with the Wind*? Then you'll remember when Rhett left Scarlet in Atlanta with her personal world once again in shambles, and she could think of nothing solid and real except Tara, the family plantation. And how the question riveted us: "What will happen next?" Then Scarlet refused to face reality, clinging to the expectation that somehow things would be better tomorrow.[1] Suddenly, there you were—at the bottom of the last page in one of the longest books you had ever read. And you couldn't believe it! What an ending!

Margaret Mitchell left the American reading public, and eventually reading publics around the world, aching for the sequel she never wrote. Perhaps she believed that any sequel to such a grand and fantastic tale of romance and dogged determination by a heroine readers passionately loved and hated was bound to be a disappointment.

Genesis ends on a much happier and more satisfying note than *Gone with the Wind,* but when you read it you know the story isn't over. Moses dropped hints that the leading characters have expectations of better days elsewhere. It's a matter of place. Similarly, as Scarlet could never be happy away from the fictionalized Tara, how much more did the people of promise need to go to their real home—to that promised strip of hilly land that the voice of God had guaranteed to Abraham, Isaac, and Jacob.

JOSEPH PRESERVED ISRAEL AND EGYPT

Through suffering the Lord had made Joseph wise, and Pharaoh had recognized this wisdom when he made Joseph administrator of the food collection and distribution system in response to the divinely forecast famine. The Spirit of God had energized Joseph's wisdom in his sanctifying encounters with his brothers when they came to Egypt with the mundane goal of buying food. Finally, Joseph directed his wisdom toward advancing the welfare of his family and the reign of Pharaoh.

From Genesis 46:1–7, describe Jacob's departure from Canaan for Egypt according to these topics:

His probable point of departure (37:14)

His final worship before leaving Canaan

God's promises at departure time

Prediction about Jacob's death (compare 46:4 with 37:35)

Jacob's entourage

From Genesis 46:8–27, describe the members of Jacob's family who went with him to Egypt at the invitation of Joseph and Pharaoh.

The number of people who went

The generations represented among the travelers

The organization of the list of Jacob's children

How this list differs from the birth order in Genesis 29 and 30

Record the numbers of descendants from each of the mothers of Jacob's children and total them.

Leah (46:15)   _____

Zilpah (46:18)   _____

Rachel (46:22)   _____

Bilhah (46:25)   _____

TOTAL   _____   (see 46:27)

In order to arrive at the number who accompanied Jacob to Egypt, subtract Er and Onan (46:12), add Dinah (v. 15), and subtract Joseph and his two sons (v. 27). The new total is _____ (see 46:26).

From Genesis 46:28–30, describe the meeting of Jacob and Joseph (notice the role of Judah).

From Genesis 46:31—47:10, describe the audience of Joseph's family with Pharaoh.

Joseph's instructions to his family about what to say

Joseph and five brothers before Pharaoh

Pharaoh's instructions to Joseph about his family

The audience between Jacob and Pharaoh

How did Joseph provide for his family in Egypt? (Gen. 47:11, 12)

What did Joseph's administration of Egypt's food supply during the famine gain for the Pharaoh in each of the following portions of Genesis 47?

vv. 13, 14

vv. 15–17

vv. 18–22

vv. 23–26

How did Jacob's growing family fare better during the famine than did the native Egyptians? (Gen. 47:11, 12, 14–26)

 FAITH ALIVE

How can wise adherence to the ways of God as revealed by His Word and Spirit lead to prosperity for a child of God, even when the times are difficult?

How can a long and intimate walk with the Lord give you confidence to face the powerful people of the world with the ease and authority that Jacob displayed in the presence of Pharaoh? (see Gen. 47:8–10)

JACOB'S FINAL BLESSING

The Lord allowed Jacob several years in which to enjoy the flourishing of his family in Egypt. When his time to die came, Jacob blessed his descendants out of a heart at peace with God and his children. The Lord had prepared Jacob through a great deal of heartache to see into the future of his offspring by means of the Holy Spirit.

What were the last years of Jacob's life like? (Gen. 47:27, 28)

What was Jacob's final arrangement with Joseph? (Gen. 47:29–31)

Where did Jacob want to be buried? (see Gen. 23:1–20; 35:27–29)

From Genesis 48:1–7, describe Jacob's plans for Joseph's sons.

The occasion of the conversation

The divine promise behind Jacob's plan

Jacob's claim about Joseph's sons

The sorrow in Jacob's love for Joseph and his sons

From Genesis 48:8–16, describe Jacob's blessing bestowed on Joseph's sons.

The standard beginning of the ritual

A similarity to a blessing years earlier (compare 48:10 with 27:1)

The tenderness between Jacob and Joseph

How Joseph took Jacob's blindness into account

How Jacob asserted his will over Joseph's

The blessing Jacob gave Joseph through his sons

From Genesis 48:17–22, describe Jacob's bestowal of a double portion of his blessing on Joseph.

Joseph's displeasure with Jacob's blessing

Jacob's explanation of his actions

Jacob's gift to Joseph

Genesis 49:1–28 records Jacob's final words to his sons in which he distills all that he has learned about them through the years and all that the Lord has revealed to him about their future.

List the sons of Jacob in the order in which they appear in the following two passages.

Genesis 46:8–25	Genesis 49:3–27
_____	_____
_____	_____
_____	_____
_____	_____
_____	_____
_____	_____
_____	_____
_____	_____
_____	_____
_____	_____
_____	_____

How does the organization of Jacob's sequence of blessing differ from the organization of the list of travelers to Egypt? (Pay attention to the mothers.)

Why did Jacob strip Reuben of his rights as firstborn son? (Gen. 49:3, 4)

Why do you think Jacob bestowed the rights of firstborn son upon Judah? (Gen. 49:8–12)

BIBLE EXTRA

"Judah" means "Praise" [see Gen. 29:35], and out of this man comes a great tribe of Israel. . . . 1) Jacob speaks important words over Judah, giving him the highest blessing. His brothers will praise him. He will triumph over all his enemies. Genesis 49:10 says that Judah will have royal authority (scepter) and legal authority (lawgiver) and will bring forth the Messiah.

2) Out of Judah, through David, comes the Christ, who in every action and detail is a praise to the Father (Luke 3:23–33). 3) The tribe of Judah (Praise) led Israel through the wilderness (Num. 2:3, 9). 4) They led in the conquest of Canaan (Judg. 1:1–19). 5) Judah is the first tribe to praise David, making him king (2 Sam. 2:1–11).[2]

From Genesis 49:3–27, summarize the meaning of Jacob's poetic predictions about each of his sons.

Reuben

Simeon and Levi (see Gen. 34:25–31)

Judah

Zebulun

Issachar

Dan

Gad

Asher

Naphtali

Joseph

Benjamin

FAITH ALIVE

If you have children or are close to some young people, try to write a blessing for each of them based on the strengths of their characters as you know them.

Consider sharing your blessings with the children as an encouragement to them.

If you do not have children, explain the concept of a blessing based on intimate knowledge of the strengths of a person's life to your parents or another very close relative and ask them to write a blessing for you.

JACOB'S FAMILY TAKES CARE OF ONE ANOTHER

The final paragraphs of the Book of Genesis portray an intimate level of fellowship and communication between the members of Jacob's family. Where there had once been suspicion and jockeying for advantage, there was openness and companionship.

What two kinds of communications did Jacob give his sons in his last conversation with them? (Gen. 49:28, 29)

Where and with whom did Jacob ask to be buried? (Gen. 49:29–32)

Describe Jacob's death. (Gen. 49:33)

From Genesis 50:1–14, describe Joseph's care of Jacob's funeral.

His personal reaction to Jacob's death

How Jacob was embalmed

Joseph's arrangements with Pharaoh

Jacob's burial ceremonies in Canaan

From Genesis 50:15–21, describe the exchange between Joseph and his brothers following the death of Jacob.

The brothers' fear

The brothers' message to Joseph

Joseph's reaction to the message

The brothers' personal appeal to Joseph

Joseph's assurance to his brothers

Do you think the confession of the brothers (Gen. 50:17) shows spiritual weakness because they did not trust Joseph's earlier assurances (Gen. 45:5–8), or do you think it shows spiritual growth because they finally verbalized their guilt to him? Give reasons for your answer.

Describe the richness of Joseph's final years in Egypt. (Gen. 50:22, 23)

What promise did Joseph make to the children of Israel in God's name before he died? (Gen. 50:24)

How did the way Joseph had his death handled express his confidence in the promise of God? (Gen. 50:25, 26)

How did Joseph's promise relate to the promise God made to Abraham in Genesis 15:13–16?

 FAITH ALIVE

Why were Jacob and his sons able to trust one another after years of suspicion and dishonesty?

What truths from the example of Jacob and his sons can you apply to your life with your family and your church to make those relationships closer?

As you look back over your study of the Book of Genesis, what spiritual lesson stands out to you as the main truth the Lord wants you to remember and how should you apply it to your life?

1. Margaret Mitchell, *Gone with the Wind* (New York: Pocket Books, Inc., 1958).
2. *Spirit-Filled Life Bible* (Nashville, TN: Thomas Nelson Publishers, 1991), 49, "Kingdom Dynamics: 'Judah' Means 'Praise.'"